THE ULTIMATE
ROCK ALBUM GUIDE

TIME-LIFE MUSIC
ALEXANDRIA, VIRGINIA

TIME-LIFE MUSIC

President: Steven L. Janas
Senior Vice President: Martin Shampaine
Vice Presidents: Jim Fishel, Donna Pickett,
              Mark Stevens, Duff Stokes
Director of New Product Development: Steven Sachs
Director of Licensing: Bonnie Pritchard
Financial Director: Michael L. Ulica
Executive Producer: Robert Hull
Project Manager: Elizabeth Riedl
Production Director: Karen Hill

Time-Life Books ia a division of
TIME LIFE INC.

TIME-LIFE CUSTOM PUBLISHING
Vice President and Publisher: Terry Newell
Vice President of Sales and Marketing: Neil Levin
Director of Special Sales: Liz Ziehl
Project Manager: Jennifer M. Lee
Managing Editor: Donia Ann Steele
Production Manager: Carolyn Clark
Quality Assurance Manager: James D. King

Book design and production by March Tenth, Inc.
Cover design by Harry Choron
Text by Tom Dupree
Research by B. George, ARChive of Contemporary Music

Library of Congress Cataloging-in-Publication Data

The Ultimate Rock Album Guide
        p. cm.
      Includes index.
      ISBN 0-7835-5285-3 (softcover)
      1. Rock music—Discography. I. Time-Life Books
      ML156.4.R6U4 1997   97-27172
      016.78166'0266—dc21   CIP
                                               MN

THE ULTIMATE ROCK ALBUM GUIDE

Editor's Note

*T*he information in this book was taken primarily from original album packages, from the Recording Industry Association of America (RIAA), and from *Billboard* magazine. In regard to *Billboard* chart information, *Top Pop Albums 1955-1996,* by Joel Whitburn (Record Research, 1996), was a valuable reference.

BILLBOARD CHART PERFORMANCE refers to *Billboard*'s Top Pop Album Chart. These entries indicate the highest chart position for the album (and, when the album made #1, the number of weeks it held that position); the date on which the album achieved its peak position; and the total number of weeks the album spent on the charts.

The highlighted title in each song list refers to the selections included in *The Time-Life Music Gold & Platinum Collection.*

All research was coordinated by the ARChive of Contemporary Music.

Introduction

very picture tells a story, Rod Stewart told us in 1971. But rock and roll fans had known that for years. From the beginning, rock albums weren't just something to listen to; they were also something to look at, something to stare at intently while listening to the music inside. For those who lived through the LP era in rock, particular cover images are forever associated not only with the music they heralded, but also with the time they represented. It's a visceral connection that affects and amplifies enjoyment of the music to this day, and it's how rock and roll became larger than life.

The album jackets represented in this collection tell a story of their own. They have reflected and influenced every aspect of popular culture. R. Crumb's brilliant illustration style, used on Big Brother and the Holding Company's *Cheap Thrills,* became a symbol of an innocent, peace-and-love hippie era, and the sixties' San Francisco concert poster motif of Van Morrison's *Blowin' Your Mind* and Cream's *Disraeli Gears* looked fresh thirty years ago, when psychedelia ruled. Only with the cynical hindsight of history does the design seem naïve, as does the cover of the Beach Boys' *Smiley Smile,* which looks as though it may have been taken from a children's picture book. In the seventies, as corporate logotypes became fashionable in the business world (and rock itself began to be recognized as a big business), album design echoed the trend: Chicago, Jimmy Buffett, Boston, the Bee Gees, Z Z Top, and many other bands created slick logos that announced the marriage of music and commerce. That relationship became even cozier in the eighties, leading to the clean, spare, advertising-design look of INXS's *Kick,* Wham!'s *Make It Big,* and Michael Jackson's *Bad.* In the nineties, when rock became truly democratized, allowing the sum of its parts to mingle in a whole new era, album art showed it all. Challenged by the reduced size of the compact disk jewel box, rock album packaging still managed to get its point across, from the raw power of Meat Loaf's amazing comeback to the quiet intimacy of Sheryl Crow's relaxed portrait.

the

*J*ust as the Beatles revolutionized the world in so many other ways, their first album cover similarly announced a change. Generally up to this point, album covers were perceived by record companies as valuable advertising space, to the point that most boasted their song lists right on the front. This one didn't—the spare photo broadcasts its subversive message of fashion and mystery louder than any clump of words possibly could.

The ornate Art Nouveau influence of the San Francisco visual-art scene, with its appropriation of turn-of-the-century flamboyance toward depiction of cult pleasures known only to the initiated, eventually made it to the covers of *Time* and *Newsweek,* but it was first seen nationwide in sixties album art. The Doors—one of the first groups to employ a recurring logotype on their album packages—feature understated but still hip-culture type for the album title on *Waiting for the Sun.* Creedence Clearwater Revival goes minimalist and makes you turn *Bayou Country* over to find out whose record it is. But the single image that best shows where album design was headed appears on Chicago's self-titled second album. The band has dispensed with most of the words in its original name, the Chicago Transit Authority. Now, there's only one word, in flowing script, treated as the corporate icon it will become. The rock band as brand name.

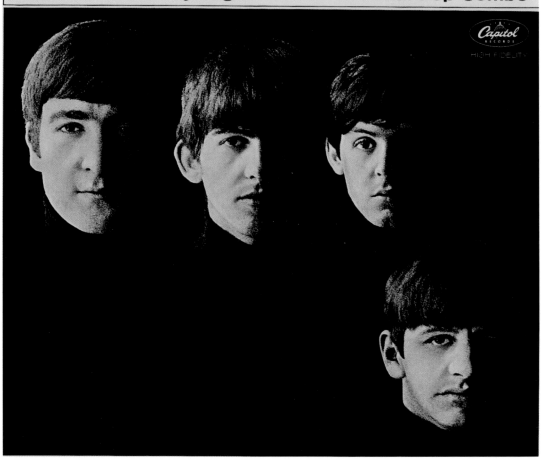

MEET THE BEATLES!

RECORD COMPANY: CAPITOL

CATALOG NUMBER: T 047

YEAR OF RELEASE: 1964

BILLBOARD CHART PERFORMANCE: #1 FOR 11 WEEKS,
FEBRUARY 1, 1964; 71 WEEKS ON CHARTS

THE BEATLES

SONGS

I WANT TO HOLD YOUR HAND

I SAW HER STANDING THERE

THIS BOY

IT WON'T BE LONG

ALL I'VE GOT TO DO

ALL MY LOVING

DON'T BOTHER ME

LITTLE CHILD

TILL THERE WAS YOU

HOLD ME TIGHT

I WANNA BE YOUR MAN

NOT A SECOND TIME

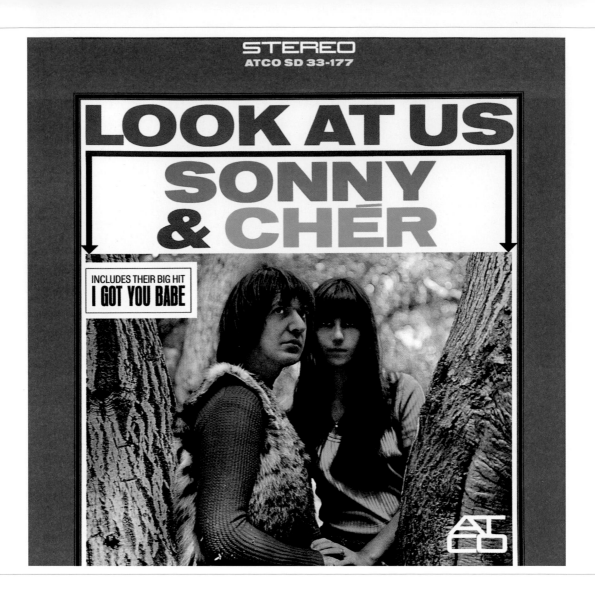

10

LOOK AT US

RECORD COMPANY: ATCO

CATALOG NUMBER: 33-177

YEAR OF RELEASE: 1965

BILLBOARD CHART PERFORMANCE: #2, AUGUST 21, 1965;

  44 WEEKS ON CHARTS

SONNY & CHER

SONGS

I GOT YOU BABE

UNCHAINED MELODY

THEN HE KISSED ME

SING C'EST LA VIE

IT'S GONNA RAIN

500 MILES

JUST YOU

THE LETTER

LET IT BE ME

YOU DON'T LOVE ME

YOU'VE REALLY GOT A HOLD ON ME

WHY DON'T THEY LET US FALL IN LOVE

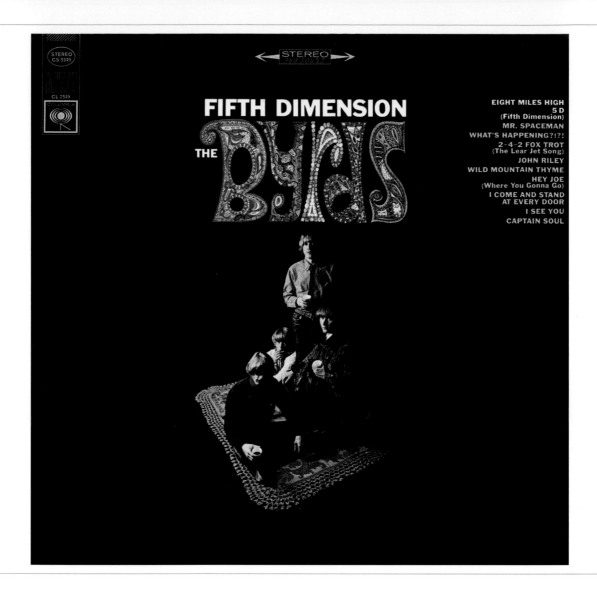

FIFTH DIMENSION

RECORD COMPANY: COLUMBIA

CATALOG NUMBER: CS 9349

YEAR OF RELEASE: 1966

BILLBOARD CHART PERFORMANCE: #24, AUGUST 27, 1966;

  28 WEEKS ON CHARTS

THE BYRDS

SONGS

5 D (FIFTH DIMENSION)

WILD MOUNTAIN THYME

MR. SPACEMAN

I SEE YOU

WHAT'S HAPPENING?!?!

I COME AND STAND AT EVERY DOOR

EIGHT MILES HIGH

HEY JOE (WHERE YOU GONNA GO)

CAPTAIN SOUL

JOHN RILEY

2—4—2 FOX TROT (THE LEAR JET SONG)

BLONDE ON BLONDE

RECORD COMPANY: COLUMBIA

CATALOG NUMBER: C2L 41

YEAR OF RELEASE: 1966

BILLBOARD CHART PERFORMANCE: #9, JULY 23, 1966;

  34 WEEKS ON CHARTS

BOB DYLAN

SONGS

RAINY DAY WOMEN #12 & 35

PLEDGING MY TIME

VISIONS OF JOHANNA

ONE OF US MUST KNOW

I WANT YOU

MEMPHIS BLUES AGAIN

LEOPARD-SKIN PILL-BOX HAT

JUST LIKE A WOMAN

MOST LIKELY YOU GO YOUR WAY AND I'LL GO MINE

TEMPORARY LIKE ACHILLES

ABSOLUTELY SWEET MARIE

4TH TIME AROUND

OBVIOUSLY 5 BELIEVERS

SAD EYED LADY OF THE LOWLANDS

SOUNDS OF SILENCE

SIMON & GARFUNKEL

RECORD COMPANY: COLUMBIA

CATALOG NUMBER: CS 9269

YEAR OF RELEASE: 1966

BILLBOARD CHART PERFORMANCE: #21, FEBRUARY 19, 1966;

  143 WEEKS ON CHARTS

SONGS

THE SOUNDS OF SILENCE

LEAVES THAT ARE GREEN

BLESSED

KATHY'S SONG

SOMEWHERE THEY CAN'T FIND ME

ANGIE

RICHARD CORY

A MOST PECULIAR MAN

APRIL COME SHE WILL

WE'VE GOT A GROOVEY THING GOIN'

I AM A ROCK

SMILEY SMILE

RECORD COMPANY: BROTHER

CATALOG NUMBER: T 9001

YEAR OF RELEASE: 1967

BILLBOARD CHART PERFORMANCE: #41, SEPTEMBER 30, 1967;

   21 WEEKS ON CHARTS

THE BEACH BOYS

SONGS

HEROES AND VILLAINS

VEGETABLES

FALL BREAKS AND BACK TO WINTER

(W. WOODPECKER SYMPHONY)

SHE'S GOIN' BALD

LITTLE PAD

GOOD VIBRATIONS

WITH ME TONIGHT

WIND CHIMES

GETTIN' HUNGRY

WONDERFUL

WHISTLE IN

DISRAELI GEARS

RECORD COMPANY: ATCO/ATLANTIC

CATALOG NUMBER: SD-33-232

YEAR OF RELEASE: 1967

BILLBOARD CHART PERFORMANCE: #4, DECEMBER 9, 1967;

  77 WEEKS ON CHARTS

CREAM

SONGS

STRANGE BREW

SUNSHINE OF YOUR LOVE

WORLD OF PAIN

DANCE THE NIGHT AWAY

BLUE CONDITION

TALES OF BRAVE ULYSSES

SWALBR

WE'RE GOING WRONG

OUTSIDE WOMAN BLUES

TAKE IT BACK

MOTHER'S LAMENT

ARE YOU EXPERIENCED

RECORD COMPANY: REPRISE/WARNER

CATALOG NUMBER: RS 6261

YEAR OF RELEASE: 1967

BILLBOARD CHART PERFORMANCE: #5, AUGUST 26, 1967;
   106 WEEKS ON CHARTS

THE JIMI HENDRIX EXPERIENCE

SONGS

PURPLE HAZE

MANIC DEPRESSION

HEY JOE

LOVE OR CONFUSION

MAY THIS BE LOVE

I DON'T LIVE TODAY

THE WIND CRIES MARY

FIRE

THIRD STONE FROM THE SUN

FOXEY LADY

ARE YOU EXPERIENCED?

SURREALISTIC PILLOW

RECORD COMPANY: RCA

CATALOG NUMBER: LSP-3766

YEAR OF RELEASE: 1967

BILLBOARD CHART PERFORMANCE: #3, MARCH 25, 1967;

   56 WEEKS ON CHARTS

JEFFERSON AIRPLANE

SONGS

SHE HAS FUNNY CARS

SOMEBODY TO LOVE

MY BEST FRIEND

TODAY

COMIN' BACK TO ME

3/5 OF A MILE IN 10 SECONDS

D.C.B.A. - 25

HOW DO YOU FEEL

EMBRYONIC JOURNEY

WHITE RABBIT

PLASTIC FANTASTIC LOVER

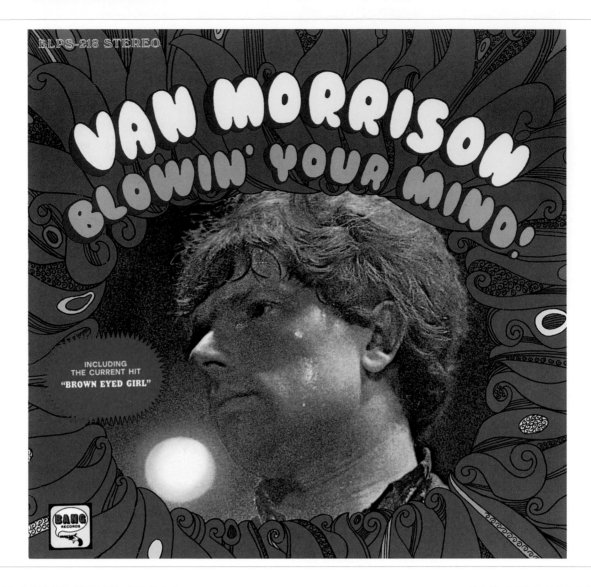

BLOWIN' YOUR MIND!

RECORD COMPANY: BANG/WEB IV

CATALOG NUMBER: BLPS-218

YEAR OF RELEASE: 1967

BILLBOARD CHART PERFORMANCE: #182, OCTOBER 7, 1967;

   7 WEEKS ON CHARTS

VAN MORRISON

SONGS

BROWN EYED GIRL

HE AIN'T GIVE YOU NONE

T. B. SHEETS

SPANISH ROSE

GOODBYE BABY (BABY GOODBYE)

RO RO ROSEY

WHO DROVE THE RED SPORTS CAR

MIDNIGHT SPECIAL

CHEAP THRILLS

RECORD COMPANY: COLUMBIA

CATALOG NUMBER: KCS 9700

YEAR OF RELEASE: 1968

BILLBOARD CHART PERFORMANCE: #1 FOR 8 WEEKS,
    AUGUST 31, 1968; 66 WEEKS ON CHARTS

BIG BROTHER & THE HOLDING COMPANY

SONGS

COMBINATION OF THE TWO

I NEED A MAN TO LOVE

SUMMERTIME

PIECE OF MY HEART

TURTLE BLUES

OH, SWEET MARY

BALL AND CHAIN

WAITING FOR THE SUN

RECORD COMPANY: ELEKTRA

CATALOG NUMBER: EKS-74024

YEAR OF RELEASE: 1968

BILLBOARD CHART PERFORMANCE: #1 FOR 4 WEEKS, AUGUST 10, 1968;

  41 WEEKS ON CHARTS

THE DOORS

SONGS

HELLO, I LOVE YOU

LOVE STREET

NOT TO TOUCH THE EARTH

SUMMER'S ALMOST GONE

WINTERTIME LOVE

THE UNKNOWN SOLDIER

SPANISH CARAVAN

MY WILD LOVE

WE COULD BE SO GOOD TOGETHER

YES, THE RIVER KNOWS

FIVE TO ONE

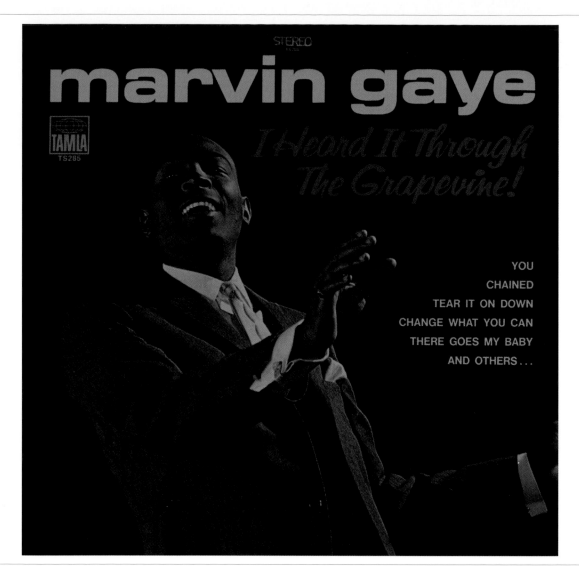

I HEARD IT THROUGH THE GRAPEVINE!

RECORD COMPANY: TAMLA/MOTOWN

CATALOG NUMBER: TS285

YEAR OF RELEASE: 1968

MARVIN GAYE

SONGS

YOU

TEAR IT ON DOWN

CHAINED

I HEARD IT THROUGH THE GRAPEVINE

AT LAST (I FOUND A LOVE)

SOME KIND OF WONDERFUL

LOVING YOU IS SWEETER THAN EVER

CHANGE WHAT YOU CAN

IT'S LOVE I NEED

EVERY NOW AND THEN

YOU'RE WHAT'S HAPPENING (IN THE WORLD TODAY)

THERE GOES MY BABY

BAYOU COUNTRY

RECORD COMPANY: FANTASY

CATALOG NUMBER: 8387

YEAR OF RELEASE: 1969

BILLBOARD CHART PERFORMANCE: #7, FEBRUARY 8, 1969;

  88 WEEKS ON CHARTS

CREEDENCE CLEARWATER REVIVAL

SONGS

BORN ON THE BAYOU

BOOTLEG

GRAVEYARD TRAIN

GOOD GOLLY MISS MOLLY

PENTHOUSE PAUPER

PROUD MARY

KEEP ON CHOOGLIN'

CROSBY, STILLS & NASH

RECORD COMPANY: ATLANTIC

CATALOG NUMBER: SD 8229

YEAR OF RELEASE: 1969

BILLBOARD CHART PERFORMANCE: #6, JUNE 28, 1969;

  107 WEEKS ON CHARTS

CROSBY, STILLS & NASH

SONGS

SUITE: JUDY BLUE EYES

MARRAKESH EXPRESS

GUINNEVERE

YOU DON'T HAVE TO CRY

PRE-ROAD DOWNS

WOODEN SHIPS

LADY OF THE ISLAND

HELPLESSLY HOPING

LONG TIME GONE

49 BYE-BYES

FROM MEMPHIS TO VEGAS/FROM VEGAS TO MEMPHIS   ELVIS PRESLEY

RECORD COMPANY: RCA/VICTOR

CATALOG NUMBER: LSP 6020

YEAR OF RELEASE: 1969

BILLBOARD CHART PERFORMANCE: #12, NOVEMBER 29, 1969;

   24 WEEKS ON CHARTS

SONGS

BLUE SUEDE SHOES	CAN'T HELP FALLING IN LOVE
JOHNNY B. GOOD	INHERIT THE WIND
ALL SHOOK UP	THIS IS THE STORY
ARE YOU LONESOME	STRANGER IN MY OWN
TONIGHT	HOME TOWN
HOUND DOG	A LITTLE BIT OF GREEN
I CAN'T STOP LOVING YOU	AND THE GRASS WON'T
MY BABE	PAY NO MIND
MEDLEY: MYSTERY TRAIN;	DO YOU KNOW WHO I AM?
TIGER MAN	FROM A JACK TO A KING
WORDS	THE FAIR'S MOVING ON
IN THE GHETTO	YOU'LL THINK OF ME
SUSPICIOUS MINDS	WITHOUT LOVE
	(THERE IS NOTHING)

24

TOMMY

THE WHO

RECORD COMPANY: DECCA/MCA

CATALOG NUMBER: DXSW 7205

YEAR OF RELEASE: 1969

BILLBOARD CHART PERFORMANCE: #4, JUNE 7, 1969;

  126 WEEKS ON CHARTS

SONGS

OVERTURE	PINBALL WIZARD
IT'S A BOY	THERE'S A DOCTOR I'VE FOUND
YOU DIDN'T HEAR IT	GO TO THE MIRROR
AMAZING JOURNEY	TOMMY CAN YOU HEAR ME
SPARKS	SMASH THE MIRROR
EYESIGHT TO THE BLIND	SENSATION
CHRISTMAS	MIRACLE CURE
COUSIN KEVIN	SALLY SIMPSON
THE ACID QUEEN	I'M FREE
UNDERTURE	WELCOME
DO YOU THINK IT'S ALRIGHT	TOMMY'S HOLIDAY CAMP
FIDDLE ABOUT	WE'RE NOT GONNA TAKE IT

the

THE ALLMAN BROTHERS BAND	IDLEWILD SOUTH
CHICAGO	CHICAGO
DEREK AND THE DOMINOS	LAYLA AND OTHER ASSORTED LOVE SONGS
GRATEFUL DEAD	THE WORKINGMAN'S DEAD
SANTANA	ABRAXAS
EMERSON, LAKE & PALMER	EMERSON, LAKE & PALMER
JANIS JOPLIN/FULL TILT BOOGIE	PEARL
CAROLE KING	TAPESTRY
ROD STEWART	EVERY PICTURE TELLS A STORY
LED ZEPPELIN	LED ZEPPELIN IV
CAT STEVENS	TEASER AND THE FIRECAT
THE WHO	WHO'S NEXT
JACKSON BROWNE	JACKSON BROWNE
ELTON JOHN	DON'T SHOOT ME I'M ONLY THE PIANO PLAYER
LOGGINS AND MESSINA	LOGGINS AND MESSINA
STEELY DAN	CAN'T BUY A THRILL
YES	FRAGILE
PAUL MCCARTNEY & WINGS	BAND ON THE RUN
STEVE MILLER BAND	THE JOKER
PAUL SIMON	THERE GOES RHYMIN' SIMON
STEVIE WONDER	INNERVISIONS
ERIC CLAPTON	461 OCEAN BOULEVARD
AEROSMITH	TOYS IN THE ATTIC
BEE GEES	MAIN COURSE
DAVID BOWIE	YOUNG AMERICANS
EAGLES	ONE OF THESE NIGHTS
JEFFERSON STARSHIP	RED OCTOPUS
BRUCE SPRINGSTEEN	BORN TO RUN
RINGO STARR	BLAST FROM YOUR PAST
BOSTON	BOSTON
BOZ SCAGGS	SILK DEGREES
DARYL HALL/JOHN OATES	BIGGER THAN BOTH OF US
HEART	DREAMBOAT ANNIE
PETER FRAMPTON	FRAMPTON COMES ALIVE
JIMMY BUFFETT	CHANGES IN LATITUDES, CHANGES IN ATTITUDES
FLEETWOOD MAC	RUMOURS
BOB MARLEY & THE WAILERS	EXODUS
QUEEN	NEWS OF THE WORLD
THE CARS	THE CARS
TOM PETTY AND THE HEARTBREAKERS	DAMN THE TORPEDOES
SUPERTRAMP	BREAKFAST IN AMERICA

*t*he seventies were the decade when the music business divested itself of the idea of the counterculture. The deadpan wandering-minstrel look of Cat Stevens's *Teaser and the Firecat* was perfectly in tune with its 1971 sensibility, but by 1979 the designers of Supertramp's *Breakfast in America* jacket were able to spoof a rose-colored age of prosperity while making no bones about the fact that they were pandering to the same commercial instincts.

Note these LP covers: Janis Joplin's one-woman dress-up party for *Pearl*, Carole King's windowsill reverie for *Tapestry*, Loggins and Messina's straightforward gaze for their second album. They all communicate honesty, as if the artist had been interrupted while just being himself. The photo on Bruce Springsteen's *Born to Run* seems to have it both ways: It's clearly a staged photo session, but the shot gives the impression that it's truly a candid moment, maybe even an outtake.

In the seventies, listeners became well aware that their music was being "packaged" for them. Now they were consumers; this was the decade that introduced corporate sponsorship of rock concerts. Some savvy designers had fun with the idea, as with Jackson Browne's *Saturate Before Using*. The design of Elton John's *Don't Shoot Me I'm Only the Piano Player* reiterates the fact that the album jacket is in essence a marquee, while winkingly alluding to Francois Truffaut's classic film *Shoot the Piano Player*. In one of David Bowie's many personas, he affects a glamorous lounge singer on the cover of *Young Americans*. A great statement on rock-as-show-business is the cover of Paul McCartney's *Band on the Run*: Though ostensibly it has a spy motif, the musicians are indeed caught in a spotlight.

Some groups elected an individual, iconic style of design outside the contemporary fray: the Eagles, Yes, the Moody Blues. As the music business became more forthcoming about having a product to sell, album design both taught and learned from a craft dedicated to making the sale: advertising.

the allman brothers band

idlewild south

IDLEWILD SOUTH

RECORD COMPANY: ATCO

CATALOG NUMBER: ATCO 342

YEAR OF RELEASE: 1970

BILLBOARD CHART PERFORMANCE: #38, DECEMBER 24, 1970;

  22 WEEKS ON CHARTS

THE ALLMAN BROTHERS BAND

SONGS

REVIVAL

DON'T KEEP ME WONDERIN'

MIDNIGHT RIDER

IN MEMORY OF ELIZABETH REED

HOOCHIE COOCHIE MAN

PLEASE CALL HOME

LEAVE MY BLUES AT HOME

CHICAGO II

RECORD COMPANY: COLUMBIA

CATALOG NUMBER: KGP 24

YEAR OF RELEASE: 1970

BILLBOARD CHART PERFORMANCE: #4, FEBRUARY 14, 1970;

  134 WEEKS ON CHARTS

CHICAGO

SONGS

MOVING IN	COLOUR MY WORLD
THE ROAD	TO BE FREE
POEM FOR THE PEOPLE	NOW MORE THAN EVER
IN THE COUNTRY	FANCY COLOURS
WAKE UP SUNSHINE (BALLET FOR A	25 OR 6 TO 4
GIRL IN BUCHANNON)	PRELUDE
MAKE ME SMILE	AM MOURNING
SO MUCH TO SAY; SO MUCH TO GIVE	PM MOURNING
ANXIETY'S MOMENT	MEMORIES OF LOVE
WEST VIRGINIA FANTASIES	IT BETTER END SOON
	WHERE DO WE GO FROM
	HERE?

LAYLA AND OTHER ASSORTED LOVE SONGS   DEREK AND THE DOMINOS

RECORD COMPANY: ATCO/ATLANTIC

CATALOG NUMBER: SD 2-704

YEAR OF RELEASE: 1970

BILLBOARD CHART PERFORMANCE: #16, NOVEMBER 21, 1970;

  65 WEEKS ON CHARTS

SONGS

I LOOKED AWAY

BELL BOTTOM BLUES

KEEP ON GROWING

NOBODY KNOWS YOU WHEN YOU'RE DOWN AND OUT

I AM YOURS

ANYDAY

KEY TO THE HIGHWAY

TELL THE TRUTH

WHY DOES LOVE GOT TO BE SO SAD?

HAVE YOU EVER LOVED A WOMAN

LITTLE WING

IT'S TOO LATE

LAYLA

THORN IN THE GARDEN

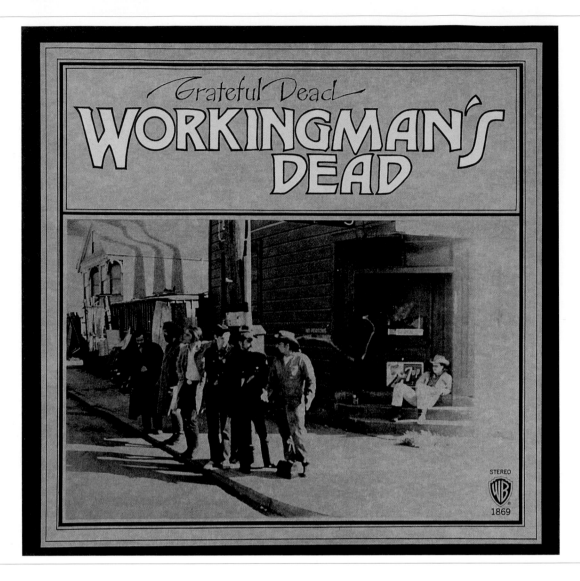

WORKINGMAN'S DEAD

RECORD COMPANY: WARNER

CATALOG NUMBER: 1869

YEAR OF RELEASE: 1970

BILLBOARD CHART PERFORMANCE: #27, JUNE 27, 1970;

26 WEEKS ON CHARTS

GRATEFUL DEAD

SONGS

UNCLE JOHN'S BAND

HIGH TIME

DIRE WOLF

NEW SPEEDWAY BOOGIE

CUMBERLAND BLUES

BLACK PETER

EASY WIND

CASEY JONES

ABRAXAS

RECORD COMPANY: COLUMBIA

CATALOG NUMBER: KC 30130

YEAR OF RELEASE: 1970

BILLBOARD CHART PERFORMANCE: #1 FOR 6 WEEKS, OCTOBER 10, 1970;

88 WEEKS ON CHARTS

SANTANA

SONGS

SINGING WINDS, CRYING BEASTS

BLACK MAGIC WOMAN / GYPSY QUEEN

OYE COMO VA

INCIDENT AT NESHABUR

SE A CABO

MOTHER'S DAUGHTER

SAMBA PA TI

HOPE YOU'RE FEELING BETTER

EL NICOYA

EMERSON, LAKE & PALMER

RECORD COMPANY: COTILLION/ATLANTIC

CATALOG NUMBER: SD 9040

YEAR OF RELEASE: 1971

BILLBOARD CHART PERFORMANCE: #18, FEBRUARY 6, 1971;

  42 WEEKS ON CHARTS

EMERSON, LAKE & PALMER

SONGS

THE BARBARIAN

TAKE A PEBBLE

KNIFE-EDGE

THE THREE FATES:

CLOTHO

LACHESIS

ATROPOS

TANK

LUCKY MAN

PEARL

JANIS JOPLIN/FULL TILT BOOGIE

RECORD COMPANY: COLUMBIA

CATALOG NUMBER: KC 30322

YEAR OF RELEASE: 1971

BILLBOARD CHART PERFORMANCE: #1 FOR 9 WEEKS, JANUARY 30, 1971;
42 WEEKS ON CHARTS

SONGS

MOVE OVER

CRY BABY

A WOMAN LEFT LONELY

HALF MOON

BURIED ALIVE IN THE BLUES

MY BABY

ME AND BOBBY MCGEE

MERCEDES BENZ

TRUST ME

GET IT WHILE YOU CAN

PE 34946

TAPESTRY

CAROLE KING

RECORD COMPANY: ODE/EPIC

CATALOG NUMBER: PE 34946

YEAR OF RELEASE: 1971

BILLBOARD CHART PERFORMANCE: #1 FOR 15 WEEKS,
   APRIL 10, 1971; 302 WEEKS ON CHARTS

SONGS

I FEEL THE EARTH MOVE

SO FAR AWAY

IT'S TOO LATE

HOME AGAIN

BEAUTIFUL

WAY OVER YONDER

YOU'VE GOT A FRIEND

WHERE YOU LEAD

WILL YOU LOVE ME TOMORROW?

SMACKWATER JACK

TAPESTRY

(YOU MAKE ME FEEL LIKE) A NATURAL WOMAN

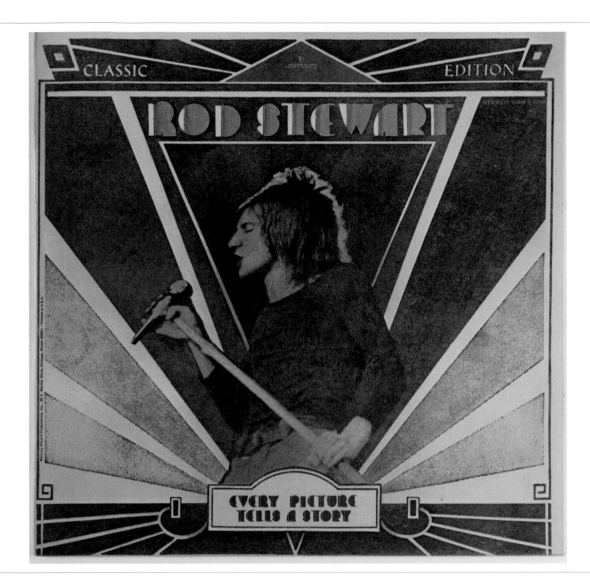

EVERY PICTURE TELLS A STORY

RECORD COMPANY: MERCURY

CATALOG NUMBER: SRM 1-609

YEAR OF RELEASE: 1971

BILLBOARD CHART PERFORMANCE: #1 FOR 4 WEEKS,
    JUNE 19, 1971; 52 WEEKS ON CHARTS

ROD STEWART

SONGS

EVERY PICTURE TELLS A STORY

SEEMS LIKE A LONG TIME

THAT'S ALL RIGHT MAMA

TOMORROW IS SUCH A LONG TIME

MAGGIE MAY

MANDOLIN WIND

(I KNOW) I'M LOSING YOU

REASON TO BELIEVE

LED ZEPPELIN IV

RECORD COMPANY: ATLANTIC

CATALOG NUMBER: SD 19129

YEAR OF RELEASE: 1971

BILLBOARD CHART PERFORMANCE: #2, NOVEMBER 27, 1971;

   259 WEEKS ON CHARTS

LED ZEPPELIN

SONGS

BLACK DOG

ROCK AND ROLL

THE BATTLE OF EVERMORE

STAIRWAY TO HEAVEN

MISTY MOUNTAIN HOP

FOUR STICKS

GOING TO CALIFORNIA

WHEN THE LEVEE BREAKS

SP 4313

TEASER AND THE FIRECAT

RECORD COMPANY: A&M

CATALOG NUMBER: SP 4313

YEAR OF RELEASE: 1971

BILLBOARD CHART PERFORMANCE: #2, OCTOBER 9, 1971;

   67 WEEKS ON CHARTS

CAT STEVENS

SONGS

THE WIND

RUBYLOVE

IF I LAUGH

CHANGES IV

HOW CAN I TELL YOU

TUESDAY'S DEAD

MORNING HAS BROKEN

BITTERBLUE

MOONSHADOW

PEACE TRAIN

40

WHO'S NEXT

RECORD COMPANY: DECCA

CATALOG NUMBER: DL7-9182

YEAR OF RELEASE: 1971

BILLBOARD CHART PERFORMANCE: #4, AUGUST 14, 1971;

  41 WEEKS ON CHARTS

THE WHO

SONGS

BABA O'RILEY

BARGAIN

LOVE AIN'T FOR KEEPING

MY WIFE

SONG IS OVER

GETTING IN TUNE

GOING MOBILE

BEHIND BLUE EYES

WON'T GET FOOLED AGAIN

Saturate Before Using

JACKSON BROWNE

LOS ANGELES, CALIFORNIA

JACKSON BROWNE

RECORD COMPANY: ASYLUM

CATALOG NUMBER: SD 5051

YEAR OF RELEASE: 1972

BILLBOARD CHART PERFORMANCE: #53, MARCH 18, 1972;

   23 WEEKS ON CHARTS

JACKSON BROWNE

SONGS

JAMAICA SAY YOU WILL

A CHILD IN THESE HILLS

SONG FOR ADAM

DOCTOR MY EYES

FROM SILVER LAKE

SOMETHING FINE

UNDER THE FALLING SKY

LOOKING INTO YOU

ROCK ME ON THE WATER

MY OPENING FAREWELL

DON'T SHOOT ME I'M ONLY THE PIANO PLAYER

ELTON JOHN

RECORD COMPANY: MCA

CATALOG NUMBER: MCA-2100

YEAR OF RELEASE: 1972

BILLBOARD CHART PERFORMANCE: #1 FOR 2 WEEKS,
 FEBRUARY 10, 1972; 89 WEEKS ON CHARTS

SONGS

DANIEL

TEACHER I NEED YOU

ELDERBERRY WINE

BLUES FOR BABY AND ME

MIDNIGHT CREEPER

HAVE MERCY ON THE CRIMINAL

I'M GOING TO BE A TEENAGE IDOL

TEXAN LOVE SONG

CROCODILE ROCK

HIGH FLYING BIRD

LOGGINS AND MESSINA

RECORD COMPANY: COLUMBIA

CATALOG NUMBER: KC 31748

YEAR OF RELEASE: 1972

BILLBOARD CHART PERFORMANCE: #16, NOVEMBER 11, 1972;

   61 WEEKS ON CHART

LOGGINS AND MESSINA

SONGS

GOOD FRIEND

WHISKEY

YOUR MAMA DON'T DANCE

LONG TAIL CAT

GOLDEN RIBBONS

THINKING OF YOU

JUST BEFORE THE NEWS

TILL THE ENDS MEET

HOLIDAY HOTEL

LADY OF MY HEART

ANGRY EYES

Stereo ABCX 758

STEELY DAN

Can't Buy A Thrill

CAN'T BUY A THRILL

RECORD COMPANY: ABC

CATALOG NUMBER: ABCX 758

YEAR OF RELEASE: 1972

BILLBOARD CHART PERFORMANCE: #17, DECEMBER 2, 1972;

   59 WEEKS ON CHARTS

STEELY DAN

SONGS

DO IT AGAIN

DIRTY WORK

KINGS

MIDNITE CRUISER

ONLY A FOOL WOULD SAY THAT

REELIN' IN THE YEARS

FIRE IN THE HOLE

BROOKLYN (OWES THE CHARMER UNDER ME)

CHANGE OF THE GUARD

TURN THAT HEARTBEAT OVER AGAIN

FRAGILE

RECORD COMPANY: ATLANTIC

CATALOG NUMBER: SD 7211

YEAR OF RELEASE: 1972

BILLBOARD CHART PERFORMANCE: #4, JANUARY 22, 1972;

  46 WEEKS ON CHARTS

YES

SONGS

ROUNDABOUT

CANS AND BRAHMS

WE HAVE HEAVEN

SOUTH SIDE OF THE SKY

FIVE PER CENT FOR NOTHING

LONG DISTANCE RUNAROUND

THE FISH

MOOD FOR A DAY

HEART OF THE SUNRISE

BAND ON THE RUN

RECORD COMPANY: APPLE

CATALOG NUMBER: SO-3415

YEAR OF RELEASE: 1973

BILLBOARD CHART PERFORMANCE: #1 FOR 4 WEEKS,

   DECEMBER 22, 1973; 116 WEEKS ON CHARTS

PAUL MCCARTNEY & WINGS

SONGS

BAND ON THE RUN

JET

BLUEBIRD

MRS. VANDERBILT

LET ME ROLL IT

MAMUNIA

NO WORDS

HELEN WHEELS

PICASSO'S LAST WORDS (DRINK TO ME)

NINETEEN HUNDRED AND EIGHTY FIVE

47

THE JOKER

RECORD COMPANY: CAPITOL/EMI

CATALOG NUMBER: SMAS 11235

YEAR OF RELEASE: 1973

BILLBOARD CHART PERFORMANCE: #2, OCTOBER 20, 1973;

   38 WEEKS ON CHARTS

STEVE MILLER BAND

SONGS

SUGAR BABE

MARY LOU

SHU BA DA DU MA MA MA MA

YOUR CASH AIN'T NOTHIN' BUT TRASH

THE JOKER

LOVIN' CUP

COME ON IN MY KITCHEN

EVIL

SOMETHING TO BELIEVE IN

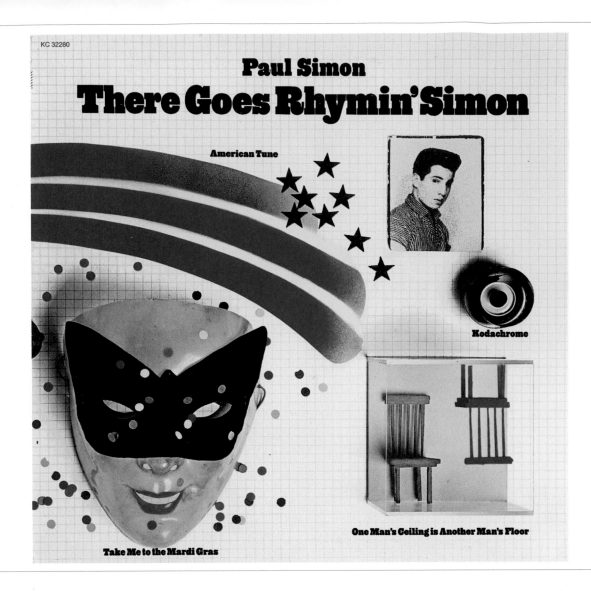

KC 32280

Paul Simon
There Goes Rhymin' Simon

American Tune

Kodachrome

One Man's Ceiling is Another Man's Floor

Take Me to the Mardi Gras

48

THERE GOES RHYMIN' SIMON

RECORD COMPANY: COLUMBIA

CATALOG NUMBER: KC 32280

YEAR OF RELEASE: 1973

BILLBOARD CHART PERFORMANCE: #2, MAY 26, 1973;

   48 WEEKS ON CHARTS

PAUL SIMON

SONGS

KODACHROME

TENDERNESS

TAKE ME TO THE MARDI GRAS

SOMETHING SO RIGHT

ONE MAN'S CEILING IS ANOTHER MAN'S FLOOR

AMERICAN TUNE

WAS A SUNNY DAY

LEARN HOW TO FALL

ST. JUDY'S COMET

LOVES ME LIKE A ROCK

INNERVISIONS

RECORD COMPANY: TAMLA

CATALOG NUMBER: T 326V1

YEAR OF RELEASE: 1973

BILLBOARD CHART PERFORMANCE: #4, AUGUST 18, 1973;

   89 WEEKS ON CHARTS

STEVIE WONDER

SONGS

TOO HIGH

VISIONS

LIVING FOR THE CITY

GOLDEN LADY

HIGHER GROUND

JESUS CHILDREN OF AMERICA

ALL IN LOVE IS FAIR

DON'T YOU WORRY 'BOUT A THING

HE'S MISSTRA KNOW-IT-ALL

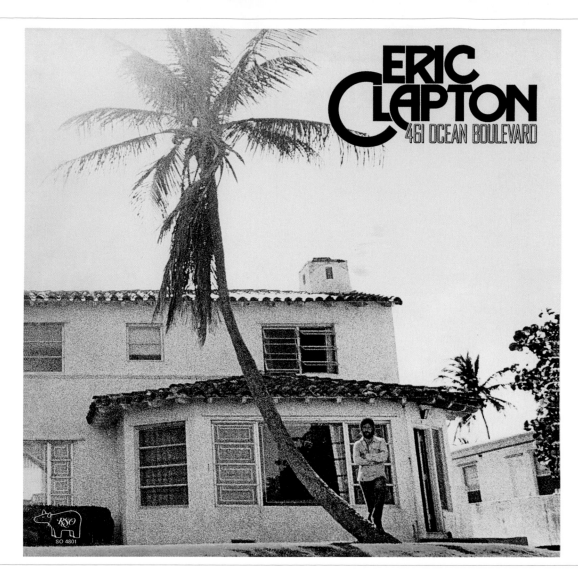

461 OCEAN BOULEVARD

RECORD COMPANY: RSO

CATALOG NUMBER: SO 4801

YEAR OF RELEASE: 1974

BILLBOARD CHART PERFORMANCE: #1 FOR 4 WEEKS,
    JULY 20, 1974; 25 WEEKS ON CHARTS

ERIC CLAPTON

SONGS

MOTHERLESS CHILDREN

GIVE ME STRENGTH

WILLIE AND THE HAND JIVE

GET READY

I SHOT THE SHERIFF

I CAN'T HOLD OUT

PLEASE BE WITH ME

LET IT GROW

STEADY ROLLIN' MAN

MAINLINE FLORIDA

TOYS IN THE ATTIC

RECORD COMPANY: COLUMBIA/CBS

CATALOG NUMBER: PCT 33479

YEAR OF RELEASE: 1975

BILLBOARD CHART PERFORMANCE: #11, APRIL 26, 1975;

   128 WEEKS ON CHARTS

AEROSMITH

SONGS

TOYS IN THE ATTIC

UNCLE SALTY

ADAM'S APPLE

WALK THIS WAY

BIG TEN INCH RECORD

SWEET EMOTION

NO MORE, NO MORE

ROUND AND ROUND

YOU SEE ME CRYING

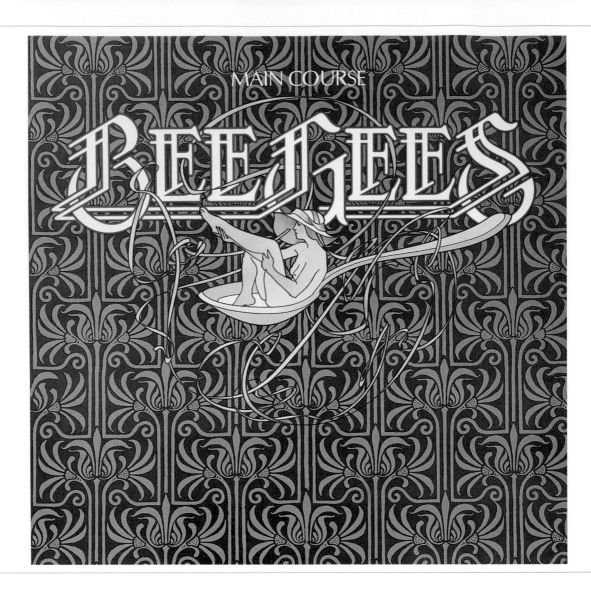

MAIN COURSE

RECORD COMPANY: RSO

CATALOG NUMBER: SO 4807

YEAR OF RELEASE: 1975

BILLBOARD CHART PERFORMANCE: #14, JUNE 21, 1975;

   74 WEEKS ON CHARTS

BEE GEES

SONGS

NIGHTS ON BROADWAY

JIVE TALKIN'

WIND OF CHANGE

SONGBIRD

FANNY (BE TENDER WITH MY LOVE)

ALL THIS MAKING LOVE

COUNTRY LANES

COME ON OVER

EDGE OF THE UNIVERSE

BABY AS YOU TURN AWAY

YOUNG AMERICANS

DAVID BOWIE

RECORD COMPANY: RCA

CATALOG NUMBER: APL1-0998

YEAR OF RELEASE: 1975

BILLBOARD CHART PERFORMANCE: #9, MARCH 22, 1975;
  51 WEEKS ON CHARTS

SONGS

YOUNG AMERICANS

WIN

FASCINATION

RIGHT

SOMEBODY UP THERE LIKES ME

ACROSS THE UNIVERSE

CAN YOU HEAR ME

FAME

ONE OF THESE NIGHTS

RECORD COMPANY: ASYLUM

CATALOG NUMBER: 7E-1039

YEAR OF RELEASE: 1975

BILLBOARD CHART PERFORMANCE: #1 FOR 5 WEEKS, JUNE 28, 1975;

  56 WEEKS ON CHARTS

EAGLES

SONGS

ONE OF THESE NIGHTS

TOO MANY HANDS

HOLLYWOOD WALTZ

JOURNEY OF THE SORCERER

LYIN' EYES

TAKE IT TO THE LIMIT

VISIONS

AFTER THE THRILL IS GONE

I WISH YOU PEACE

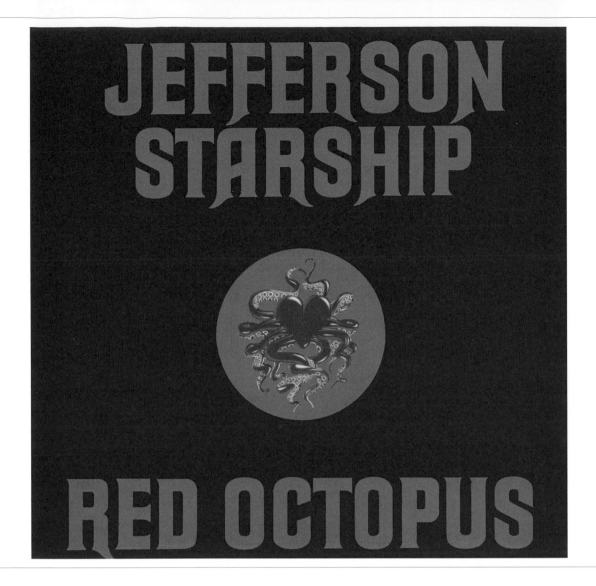

RED OCTOPUS

RECORD COMPANY: GRUNT

CATALOG NUMBER: BFL1-0999

YEAR OF RELEASE: 1975

BILLBOARD CHART PERFORMANCE: #1 FOR 4 WEEKS,

    JULY 19, 1975; 87 WEEKS ON CHARTS

JEFFERSON STARSHIP

SONGS

FAST BUCK FREDDIE

MIRACLES

GIT FIDDLER

AI GARIMASŪ (THERE IS LOVE)

SWEETER THAN HONEY

PLAY ON LOVE

TUMBLIN

I WANT TO SEE ANOTHER WORLD

SANDALPHON

THERE WILL BE LOVE

BORN TO RUN

RECORD COMPANY: COLUMBIA

CATALOG NUMBER: PC 33795

YEAR OF RELEASE: 1975

BILLBOARD CHART PERFORMANCE: #3, SEPTEMBER 13, 1975;

  110 WEEKS ON CHARTS

BRUCE SPRINGSTEEN

SONGS

THUNDER ROAD

TENTH AVENUE FREEZE-OUT

NIGHT

BACKSTREETS

BORN TO RUN

SHE'S THE ONE

MEETING ACROSS THE RIVER

JUNGLELAND

BLAST FROM YOUR PAST
RINGO STARR

You're Sixteen
No No Song
It Don't Come Easy
Photograph
Back Off Boogaloo

Only You (And You Alone)
Beaucoups Of Blues
Oh My My
Early 1970
I'm The Greatest

BLAST FROM YOUR PAST

RECORD COMPANY: CAPITOL

CATALOG NUMBER: SW 3422

YEAR OF RELEASE: 1975

BILLBOARD CHART PERFORMANCE: #30, DECEMBER 6, 1975;

11 WEEKS ON CHARTS

RINGO STARR

SONGS

YOU'RE SIXTEEN

NO NO SONG

IT DON'T COME EASY

PHOTOGRAPH

BACK OFF BOOGALOO

ONLY YOU (AND YOU ALONE)

BEAUCOUPS OF BLUES

OH MY MY

EARLY 1970

I'M THE GREATEST

BOSTON

RECORD COMPANY: EPIC

CATALOG NUMBER: 34188

YEAR OF RELEASE: 1976

BILLBOARD CHART PERFORMANCE: #3, SEPTEMBER 25, 1976;

   132 WEEKS ON CHARTS

BOSTON

SONGS

MORE THAN A FEELING

PEACE OF MIND

FOREPLAY / LONG TIME

ROCK AND ROLL BAND

SMOKIN'

HITCH A RIDE

SOMETHING ABOUT YOU

LET ME TAKE YOU HOME TONIGHT

BOZ SCAGGS

SILK DEGREES

RECORD COMPANY: COLUMBIA

CATALOG NUMBER: 33920

YEAR OF RELEASE: 1976

BILLBOARD CHART PERFORMANCE: #2, MARCH 20, 1976;

   115 WEEKS ON CHARTS

BOZ SCAGGS

SONGS

WHAT CAN I SAY

GEORGIA

JUMP STREET

WHAT DO YOU WANT THE GIRL TO DO

HARBOR LIGHTS

LOWDOWN

IT'S OVER

LOVE ME TOMORROW

LIDO SHUFFLE

WE'RE ALL ALONE

APL1-1467

BIGGER THAN BOTH OF US

RECORD COMPANY: RCA

CATALOG NUMBER: APL1-1467

YEAR OF RELEASE: 1976

BILLBOARD CHART PERFORMANCE: #13, AUGUST 28, 1976;

  57 WEEKS ON CHARTS

DARYL HALL/JOHN OATES

SONGS

BACK TOGETHER AGAIN

RICH GIRL

CRAZY EYES

DO WHAT YOU WANT, BE WHAT YOU ARE

KERRY

LONDON LUCK, AND LOVE

ROOM TO BREATHE

YOU'LL NEVER LEARN

FALLING

DREAMBOAT ANNIE

RECORD COMPANY: MUSHROOM

CATALOG NUMBER: MRS-5005

YEAR OF RELEASE: 1976

BILLBOARD CHART PERFORMANCE: #7, APRIL 10, 1976;

   100 WEEKS ON CHARTS

HEART

SONGS

MAGIC MAN

DREAMBOAT ANNIE (FANTASY CHILD)

CRAZY ON YOU

SOUL OF THE SEA

DREAMBOAT ANNIE

WHITE LIGHTNING AND WINE

(LOVE ME LIKE MUSIC) I'LL BE YOUR SONG

SING CHILD

HOW DEEP IT GOES

DREAMBOAT ANNIE (REPRISE)

Frampton Comes Alive!

FRAMPTON COMES ALIVE

PETER FRAMPTON

RECORD COMPANY: A&M

CATALOG NUMBER: SP-3703

YEAR OF RELEASE: 1976

BILLBOARD CHART PERFORMANCE: #1 FOR 10 WEEKS,
JANUARY 31, 1976; 97 WEEKS ON CHARTS

SONGS

SOMETHING'S HAPPENING

DOOBIE WAH

SHOW ME THE WAY

IT'S A PLAIN SHAME

ALL I WANT TO BE

(IS BY YOUR SIDE)

WIND OF CHANGE

BABY, I LOVE YOUR WAY

I WANNA GO TO THE SUN

PENNY FOR YOUR THOUGHTS

(I'LL GIVE YOU) MONEY

SHINE ON

JUMPING JACK FLASH

LINES ON MY FACE

DO YOU FEEL LIKE WE DO

CHANGES IN LATITUDES, CHANGES IN ATTITUDES

JIMMY BUFFETT

RECORD COMPANY: ABC

CATALOG NUMBER: AB-990

YEAR OF RELEASE: 1977

BILLBOARD CHART PERFORMANCE: #12, FEBRUARY 12, 1977;

  42 WEEKS ON CHARTS

RUMOURS

RECORD COMPANY: WARNER

CATALOG NUMBER: BSK 3010

YEAR OF RELEASE: 1977

BILLBOARD CHART PERFORMANCE: #1 FOR 31 WEEKS,

   FEBRUARY 26, 1977; 134 WEEKS ON CHARTS

FLEETWOOD MAC

SONGS

SECOND HAND NEWS

DREAMS

NEVER GOING BACK AGAIN

DON'T STOP

GO YOUR OWN WAY

SONGBIRD

THE CHAIN

YOU MAKE LOVING FUN

I DON'T WANT TO KNOW

OH DADDY

GOLD DUST WOMAN

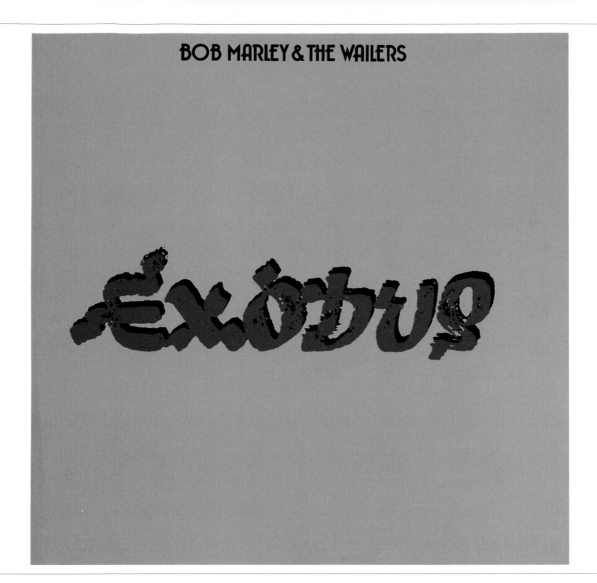

BOB MARLEY & THE WAILERS

Exodus

65

EXODUS

RECORD COMPANY: ISLAND

CATALOG NUMBER: 90034-1

YEAR OF RELEASE: 1977

BILLBOARD CHART PERFORMANCE: #20, JUNE 11, 1977;

   24 WEEKS ON CHARTS

BOB MARLEY & THE WAILERS

SONGS

NATURAL MYSTIC

SO MUCH THINGS TO SAY

GUILTINESS

THE HEATHEN

EXODUS

JAMMING

WAITING IN VAIN

TURN YOUR LIGHTS DOWN LOW

THREE LITTLE BIRDS

ONE LOVE / PEOPLE GET READY

NEWS OF THE WORLD

QUEEN

RECORD COMPANY: ELEKTRA

CATALOG NUMBER: 6E-112

YEAR OF RELEASE: 1977

BILLBOARD CHART PERFORMANCE: #3, NOVEMBER 26, 1977;

   37 WEEKS ON CHARTS

SONGS

WE WILL ROCK YOU

WE ARE THE CHAMPIONS

SHEER HEART ATTACK

ALL DEAD ALL DEAD

SPREAD YOUR WINGS

FIGHT FROM THE INSIDE

GET DOWN MAKE LOVE

SLEEPING ON THE SIDEWALK

WHO NEEDS YOU

IT'S LATE

MY MELANCHOLY BLUES

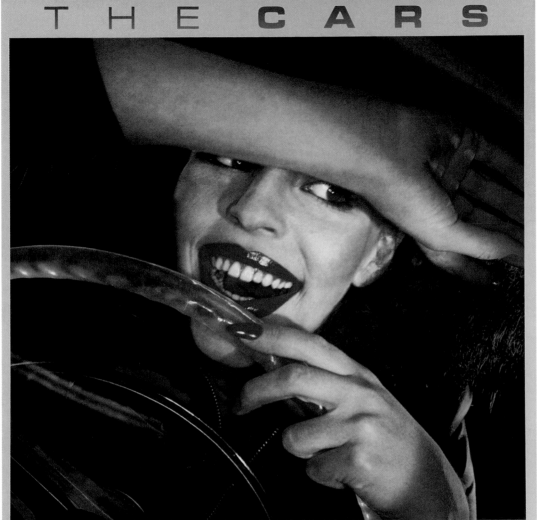

THE CARS

THE CARS

RECORD COMPANY: ELEKTRA

CATALOG NUMBER: 6E-135

YEAR OF RELEASE: 1978

BILLBOARD CHART PERFORMANCE: #18, JULY 1, 1978;

    139 WEEKS ON CHARTS

THE CARS

SONGS

GOOD TIMES ROLL

MY BEST FRIEND'S GIRL

JUST WHAT I NEEDED

I'M IN TOUCH WITH YOUR WORLD

DON'T CHA STOP

YOU'RE ALL I'VE GOT TONIGHT

BYE BYE LOVE

MOVING IN STEREO

ALL MIXED UP

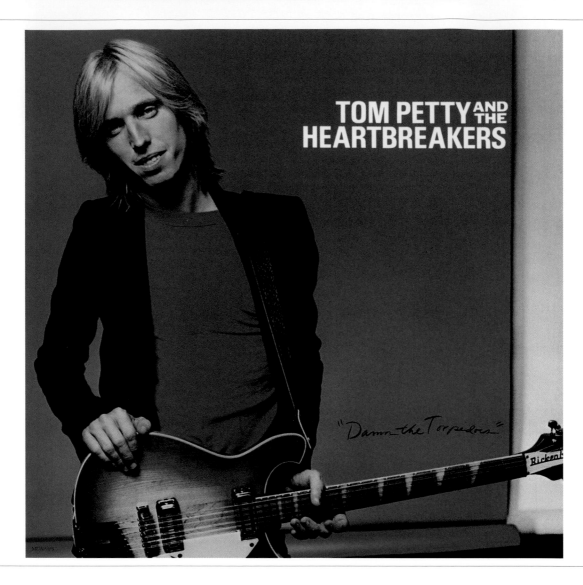

DAMN THE TORPEDOES

TOM PETTY AND THE HEARTBREAKERS

RECORD COMPANY: BACKSTREET/MCA

CATALOG NUMBER: MCA-5105

YEAR OF RELEASE: 1979

BILLBOARD CHART PERFORMANCE: #2, NOVEMBER 10, 1979;

  66 WEEKS ON CHARTS

SONGS

REFUGEE

HERE COMES MY GIRL

EVEN THE LOSERS

SHADOW OF A DOUBT (A COMPLEX KID)

CENTURY CITY

DON'T DO ME LIKE THAT

YOU TELL ME

WHAT ARE YOU DOIN' IN MY LIFE?

LOUISIANA RAIN

BREAKFAST IN AMERICA

RECORD COMPANY: A&M

CATALOG NUMBER: SP-3708

YEAR OF RELEASE: 1979

BILLBOARD CHART PERFORMANCE: #1 FOR 6 WEEKS,

    MARCH 31, 1979; 88 WEEKS ON CHARTS

SUPERTRAMP

SONGS

GONE HOLLYWOOD

THE LOGICAL SONG

GOODBYE STRANGER

BREAKFAST IN AMERICA

OH DARLING

TAKE THE LONG WAY HOME

LORD IS IT MINE

JUST ANOTHER NERVOUS WRECK

CASUAL CONVERSATIONS

CHILD OF VISION

the 80s

BLONDIE	AUTOAMERICAN
BILLY JOEL	GLASS HOUSES
JOHN LENNON/YOKO ONO	DOUBLE FANTASY
PHIL COLLINS	FACE VALUE
THE GO-GO'S	BEAUTY AND THE BEAT
GEORGE HARRISON	SOMEWHERE IN ENGLAND
JOURNEY	ESCAPE
STEVIE NICKS	BELLA DONNA
REO SPEEDWAGON	HI INFIDELITY
JOHN COUGAR	AMERICAN FOOL
MICHAEL JACKSON	THRILLER
DURAN DURAN	SEVEN AND THE RAGGED TIGER
CYNDI LAUPER	SHE'S SO UNUSUAL
THE PRETENDERS	LEARNING TO CRAWL
THE POLICE	SYNCHRONICITY
ZZ TOP	ELIMINATOR
BRUCE SPRINGSTEEN	BORN IN THE U.S.A.
TINA TURNER	PRIVATE DANCER
WHAM!	MAKE IT BIG
BRYAN ADAMS	RECKLESS
DIRE STRAITS	BROTHERS IN ARMS
EURYTHMICS	BE YOURSELF TONIGHT
STING	THE DREAM OF THE BLUE TURTLES
BON JOVI	SLIPPERY WHEN WET
GENESIS	INVISIBLE TOUCH
BRUCE HORNSBY AND THE RANGE	THE WAY IT IS
JANET JACKSON	CONTROL
HUEY LEWIS AND THE NEWS	FORE!
VAN HALEN	5150
STEVE WINWOOD	BACK IN THE HIGH LIFE
DEF LEPPARD	HYSTERIA
GRATEFUL DEAD	IN THE DARK
INXS	KICK
MICHAEL JACKSON	BAD
GEORGE MICHAEL	FAITH
SIMPLE MINDS	LIVE IN THE CITY OF LIGHT
U2	THE JOSHUA TREE
THE B-52'S	COSMIC THING
FINE YOUNG CANNIBALS	THE RAW & THE COOKED
DON HENLEY	THE END OF THE INNOCENCE
MADONNA	LIKE A PRAYER
TEARS FOR FEARS	SOWING THE SEEDS OF LOVE

TV's instant national spotlight made an act's visual appearance as critical as its sound, and album designers rushed to help record buyers make the connection. The photo for *Seven and the Ragged Tiger*, by Duran Duran, one of the first bands made popular by music videos, looks like it could have been shot on a video set. *She's So Unusual*, by Cyndi Lauper, also trades on the singer's eccentric video persona, as does the cover of *Eurythmics*, which goes so far as to suggest Annie Lennox as seen on a TV screen. And the Go-Go's might be getting ready for a video session in their hilarious photo for *Beauty and the Beat*.

MTV had yet another effect. It wasn't lost on the designers that one watched music videos through a sea of commercials. And so advertising became part of the experience. The designs for Michael Jackson's *Bad* and INXS's *Kick* seemed fresh in the eighties; they looked more like ads than album covers. So did Janet Jackson's *Control*, with its suggestion of fashion layouts and kinetic animation. Both the dramatic photo and the powerful type design on George Michael's *Faith* were clearly inspired by advertising.

The eighties were also the decade in which the compact disk edged vinyl albums out of the record store, taking the foot-square LP canvas away from rock designers forever. Album designers in the eighties had to change their styles to accommodate an industry that had undergone nothing less than a complete metamorphosis—right down to the size of the racks in the record stores.

AUTOAMERICAN

RECORD COMPANY: CHRYSALIS

CATALOG NUMBER: CHE 1290

YEAR OF RELEASE: 1980

BILLBOARD CHART PERFORMANCE: #7, DECEMBER 13, 1980;

   34 WEEKS ON CHARTS

BLONDIE

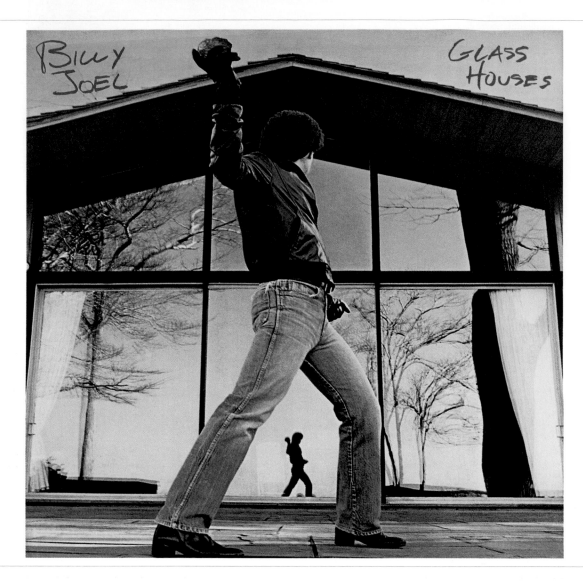

GLASS HOUSES

RECORD COMPANY: COLUMBIA

CATALOG NUMBER: FC 36384

YEAR OF RELEASE: 1980

BILLBOARD CHART PERFORMANCE: #1 FOR 6 WEEKS,

   MARCH 22, 1980; 73 WEEKS ON CHARTS

BILLY JOEL

SONGS

YOU MAY BE RIGHT

SOMETIMES A FANTASY

DON'T ASK ME WHY

IT'S STILL ROCK AND ROLL TO ME

ALL FOR LEYNA

I DON'T WANT TO BE ALONE

SLEEPING WITH THE TELEVISION ON

C'ETAIT TOI (YOU WERE THE ONE)

CLOSE TO THE BORDERLINE

THROUGH THE LONG NIGHT

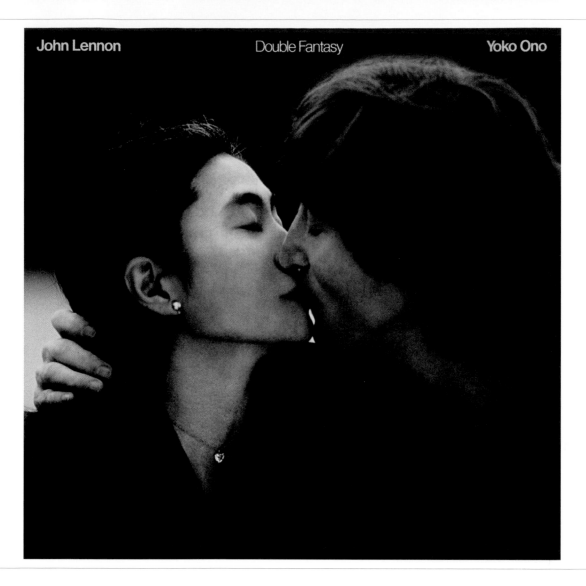

DOUBLE FANTASY

RECORD COMPANY: GEFFEN

CATALOG NUMBER: GHS 2001

YEAR OF RELEASE: 1980

BILLBOARD CHART PERFORMANCE: #1 FOR 8 WEEKS,
   DECEMBER 6, 1980; 74 WEEKS ON CHARTS

JOHN LENNON/YOKO ONO

SONGS

(JUST LIKE) STARTING OVER

KISS KISS KISS

CLEANUP TIME

GIVE ME SOMETHING

I'M LOSING YOU

I'M MOVING ON

BEAUTIFUL BOY (DARLING BOY)

WATCHING THE WHEELS

I'M YOUR ANGEL

WOMAN

BEAUTIFUL BOYS

DEAR YOKO

EVERY MAN HAS A WOMAN WHO LOVES HIM

HARD TIMES ARE OVER

Face Value   Phil Collins

FACE VALUE

RECORD COMPANY: ATLANTIC

CATALOG NUMBER: SD 16029

YEAR OF RELEASE: 1981

BILLBOARD CHART PERFORMANCE: #7, MARCH 14, 1981;

   164 WEEKS ON CHARTS

PHIL COLLINS

SONGS

IN THE AIR TONIGHT

THIS MUST BE LOVE

BEHIND THE LINES

THE ROOF IS LEAKING

DRONED

HAND IN HAND

I MISSED AGAIN

YOU KNOW WHAT I MEAN

THUNDER AND LIGHTNING

I'M NOT MOVING

IF LEAVING ME IS EASY

TOMORROW NEVER KNOWS

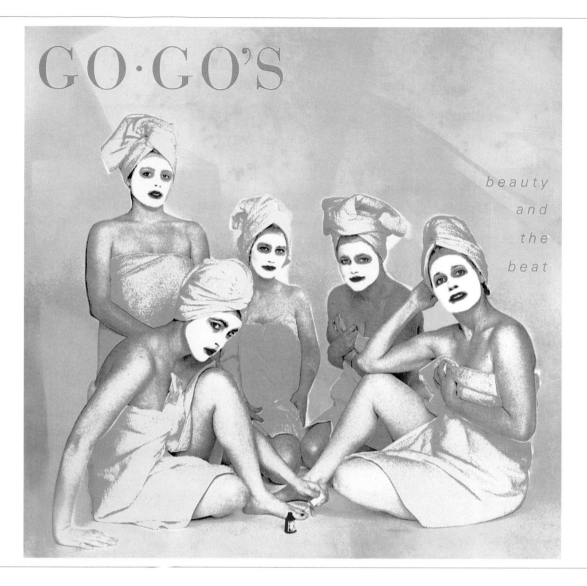

BEAUTY AND THE BEAT

RECORD COMPANY: I.R.S.

CATALOG NUMBER: SP 70021

YEAR OF RELEASE: 1981

BILLBOARD CHART PERFORMANCE: #1 FOR 6 WEEKS,

AUGUST 1, 1981; 72 WEEKS ON CHARTS

THE GO-GO'S

SONGS

OUR LIPS ARE SEALED

HOW MUCH MORE

TONITE

LUST TO LOVE

THIS TOWN

WE GOT THE BEAT

FADING FAST

AUTOMATIC

YOU CAN'T WALK IN YOUR SLEEP

(IF YOU CAN'T SLEEP)

SKIDMARKS ON MY HEART

CAN'T STOP THE WORLD

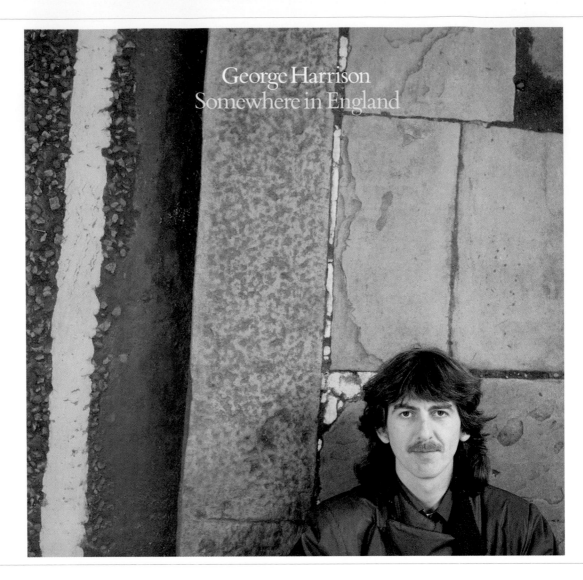

George Harrison
Somewhere in England

SOMEWHERE IN ENGLAND

RECORD COMPANY: DARK HORSE

CATALOG NUMBER: DHK 3492

YEAR OF RELEASE: 1981

BILLBOARD CHART PERFORMANCE: #11, JUNE 20, 1981;

13 WEEKS ON CHARTS

GEORGE HARRISON

SONGS

BLOOD FROM A CLONE

UNCONSCIOUSNESS RULES

LIFE ITSELF

ALL THOSE YEARS AGO

BALTIMORE ORIOLE

TEARDROPS

THAT WHICH I HAVE LOST

WRITING'S ON THE WALL

HONG KONG BLUES

SAVE THE WORLD

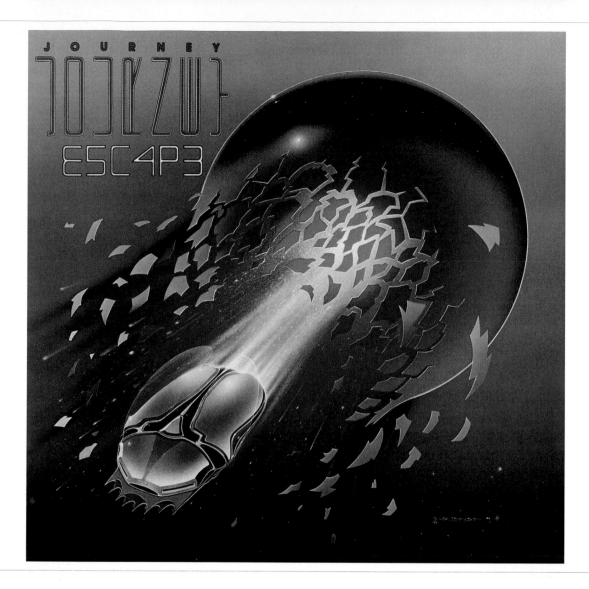

ESCAPE

RECORD COMPANY: CBS/COLUMBIA

CATALOG NUMBER: TC 37408

YEAR OF RELEASE: 1981

BILLBOARD CHART PERFORMANCE: #1 FOR ONE WEEK,
    AUGUST 8, 1981; 146 WEEKS ON CHARTS

JOURNEY

SONGS

DON'T STOP BELIEVIN'

STONE IN LOVE

WHO'S CRYING NOW

KEEP ON RUNNIN'

STILL THEY RIDE

ESCAPE

LAY IT DOWN

DEAD OR ALIVE

MOTHER, FATHER

OPEN ARMS

BELLA DONNA

RECORD COMPANY: MODERN

CATALOG NUMBER: MR 38-139

YEAR OF RELEASE: 1981

BILLBOARD CHART PERFORMANCE: #1 FOR ONE WEEK,

   AUGUST 15, 1981; 141 WEEKS ON CHARTS

STEVIE NICKS

SONGS

BELLA DONNA

KIND OF WOMAN

STOP DRAGGIN' MY HEART AROUND

THINK ABOUT IT

AFTER THE GLITTER FADES

EDGE OF SEVENTEEN

HOW STILL MY LOVE

LEATHER AND LACE

OUTSIDE THE RAIN

THE HIGHWAYMAN

HI INFIDELITY

RECORD COMPANY: EPIC

CATALOG NUMBER: 36844

YEAR OF RELEASE: 1981

BILLBOARD CHART PERFORMANCE: #1 FOR 15 WEEKS,

DECEMBER 13, 1981; 101 WEEKS ON CHARTS

REO SPEEDWAGON

SONGS

DON'T LET HIM GO

KEEP ON LOVING YOU

FOLLOW MY HEART

IN YOUR LETTER

TAKE IT ON THE RUN

TOUGH GUYS

OUT OF SEASON

SHAKIN' IT LOOSE

SOMEONE TONIGHT

I WISH YOU WERE THERE

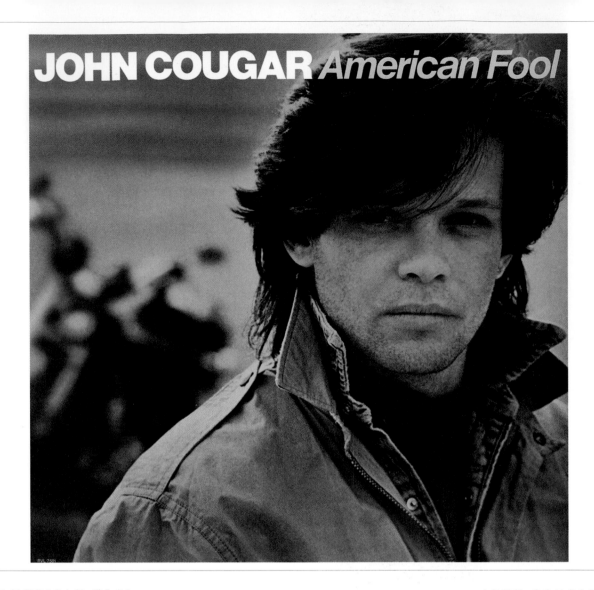

AMERICAN FOOL

RECORD COMPANY: RIVA/POLYGRAM

CATALOG NUMBER: RVL 7501

YEAR OF RELEASE: 1982

BILLBOARD CHART PERFORMANCE: #1 FOR 9 WEEKS,

   MAY 8, 1982; 120 WEEKS ON CHARTS

JOHN COUGAR

SONGS

HURTS SO GOOD

JACK AND DIANE

HAND TO HOLD ON TO

DANGER LIST

CAN YOU TAKE IT

THUNDERING HEARTS

CHINA GIRL

CLOSE ENOUGH

WEAKEST MOMENTS

THRILLER

RECORD COMPANY: EPIC

CATALOG NUMBER: QE-38112

YEAR OF RELEASE: 1982

BILLBOARD CHART PERFORMANCE: #1 FOR 37 WEEKS,

  DECEMBER 25, 1982; 122 WEEKS ON CHARTS

MICHAEL JACKSON

SONGS

WANNA BE STARTIN' SOMETHIN'

BABY BE MINE

THE GIRL IS MINE

THRILLER

BEAT IT

BILLIE JEAN

HUMAN NATURE

P. Y. T. (PRETTY YOUNG THING)

THE LADY IN MY LIFE

SEVEN AND THE RAGGED TIGER

RECORD COMPANY: CAPITOL

CATALOG NUMBER: ST 12310

YEAR OF RELEASE: 1983

BILLBOARD CHART PERFORMANCE: #8, DECEMBER 10, 1983;

    64 WEEKS ON CHARTS

DURAN DURAN

SONGS

THE REFLEX

NEW MOON ON MONDAY

(I'M LOOKING FOR) CRACKS IN THE PAVEMENT

I TAKE THE DICE

OF CRIME AND PASSION

UNION OF THE SNAKE

SHADOWS ON YOUR SIDE

TIGER TIGER

THE SEVENTH STRANGER

SHE'S SO UNUSUAL

RECORD COMPANY: PORTRAIT

CATALOG NUMBER: BFR 38930

YEAR OF RELEASE: 1983

BILLBOARD CHART PERFORMANCE: # 4, DECEMBER 24, 1983;

   96 WEEKS ON CHARTS

CYNDI LAUPER

SONGS

MONEY CHANGES EVERYTHING

GIRLS JUST WANT TO HAVE FUN

WHEN YOU WERE MINE

TIME AFTER TIME

SHE BOP

ALL THROUGH THE NIGHT

WITNESS

I'LL KISS YOU

HE'S SO UNUSUAL

YEAH YEAH

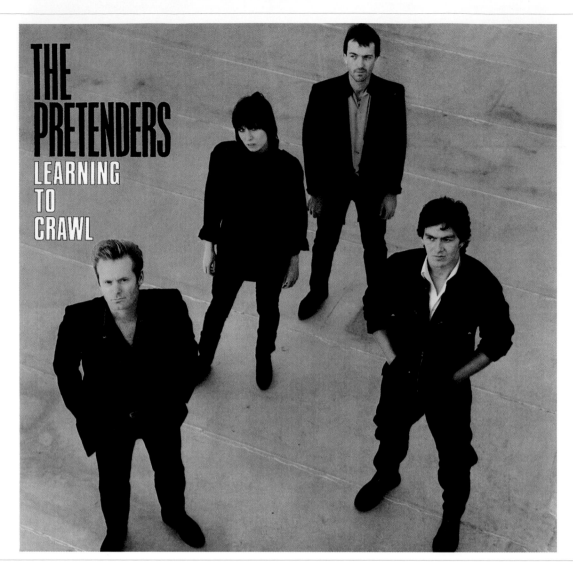

LEARNING TO CRAWL

RECORD COMPANY: SIRE

CATALOG NUMBER: 23980

YEAR OF RELEASE: 1983

BILLBOARD CHART PERFORMANCE: #5, FEBRUARY 4, 1984;

  42 WEEKS ON CHARTS

THE PRETENDERS

SONGS

MIDDLE OF THE ROAD

BACK ON THE CHAIN GANG

TIME THE AVENGER

WATCHING THE CLOTHES

SHOW ME

THUMBELINA

MY CITY WAS GONE

THIN LINE BETWEEN LOVE AND HATE

I HURT YOU

2000 MILES

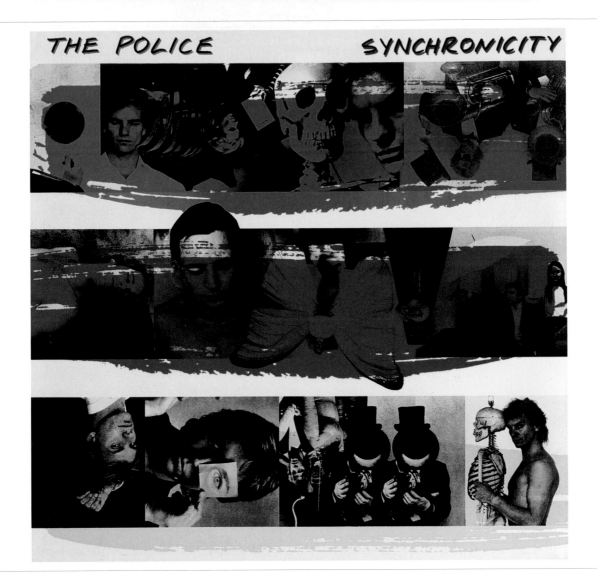

THE POLICE — SYNCHRONICITY

SYNCHRONICITY

RECORD COMPANY: A&M

CATALOG NUMBER: SP-3735

YEAR OF RELEASE: 1983

BILLBOARD CHART PERFORMANCE: #1 FOR 17 WEEKS,
   JULY 2, 1983; 75 WEEKS ON CHARTS

THE POLICE

SONGS

SYNCHRONICITY I

WALKING IN YOUR FOOTSTEPS

O MY GOD

MOTHER

MISS GRADENKO

SYNCHRONICITY II

EVERY BREATH YOU TAKE

KING OF PAIN

WRAPPED AROUND YOUR FINGER

TEA IN THE SAHARA

ELIMINATOR

RECORD COMPANY: WARNER

CATALOG NUMBER: 23774

YEAR OF RELEASE: 1983

BILLBOARD CHART PERFORMANCE: #9, APRIL 23, 1983;

  183 WEEKS ON CHARTS

ZZ TOP

SONGS

GIMME ALL YOUR LOVIN

GOT ME UNDER PRESSURE

SHARP DRESSED MAN

I NEED YOU TONIGHT

I GOT THE SIX

LEGS

THUG

TV DINNERS

DIRTY DOG

IF I COULD ONLY FLAG HER DOWN

BAD GIRL

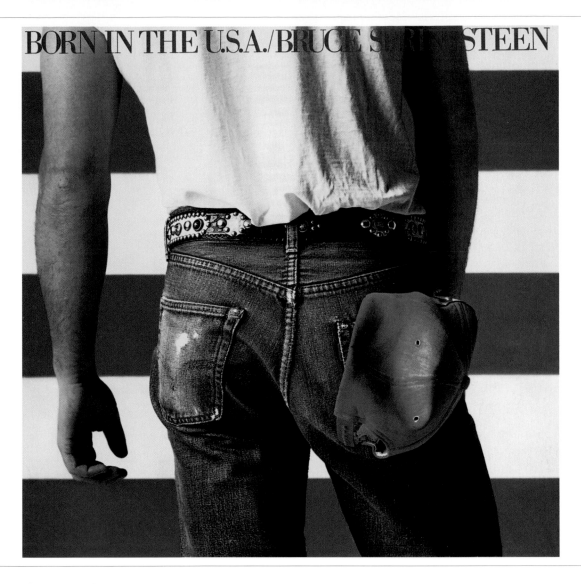

BORN IN THE U.S.A./BRUCE SPRINGSTEEN

BORN IN THE U.S.A.

RECORD COMPANY: COLUMBIA

CATALOG NUMBER: OC 38653

YEAR OF RELEASE: 1984

BILLBOARD CHART PERFORMANCE: #1 FOR 7 WEEKS,

   JUNE 23, 1984; 139 WEEKS ON CHARTS

BRUCE SPRINGSTEEN

SONGS

BORN IN THE U.S.A.

COVER ME

DARLINGTON COUNTY

WORKING ON THE HIGHWAY

DOWNBOUND TRAIN

I'M ON FIRE

NO SURRENDER

BOBBY JEAN

I'M GOIN' DOWN

GLORY DAYS

DANCING IN THE DARK

MY HOMETOWN

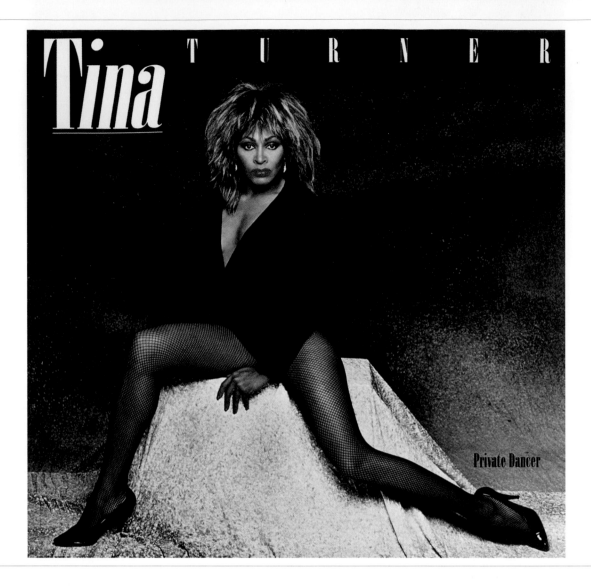

PRIVATE DANCER

RECORD COMPANY: CAPITOL/EMI

CATALOG NUMBER: ST-12330

YEAR OF RELEASE: 1984

BILLBOARD CHART PERFORMANCE: #3, JUNE 16, 1984;

   106 WEEKS ON CHARTS

TINA TURNER

SONGS

I MIGHT HAVE BEEN QUEEN

WHAT'S LOVE GOT TO DO WITH IT

SHOW SOME RESPECT

I CAN'T STAND THE RAIN

BETTER BE GOOD TO ME

LET'S STAY TOGETHER

1984

STEEL CLAW

PRIVATE DANCER

MAKE IT BIG

RECORD COMPANY: COLUMBIA

CATALOG NUMBER: FC 39595

YEAR OF RELEASE: 1984

BILLBOARD CHART PERFORMANCE: #1 FOR 3 WEEKS,

   NOVEMBER 10, 1984; 80 WEEKS ON CHARTS

WHAM!

SONGS

WAKE ME UP BEFORE YOU GO-GO

EVERYTHING SHE WANTS

HEARTBEAT

LIKE A BABY

FREEDOM

IF YOU WERE THERE

CREDIT CARD BABY

CARELESS WHISPER

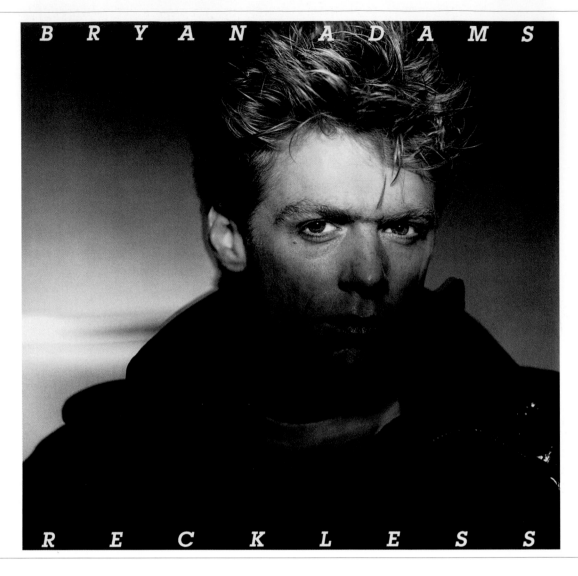

RECKLESS

RECORD COMPANY: A&M

CATALOG NUMBER: SP-5013

YEAR OF RELEASE: 1985

BILLBOARD CHART PERFORMANCE: #1 FOR 2 WEEKS,
   NOVEMBER 24, 1985; 83 WEEKS ON CHARTS

BRYAN ADAMS

SONGS

ONE NIGHT LOVE AFFAIR

SHE'S ONLY HAPPY WHEN SHE'S DANCIN'

RUN TO YOU

HEAVEN

SOMEBODY

SUMMER OF '69

KIDS WANNA ROCK

IT'S ONLY LOVE

LONG GONE

AIN'T GONNA CRY

93

BROTHERS IN ARMS

DIRE STRAITS

RECORD COMPANY: WARNER

CATALOG NUMBER: 25264

YEAR OF RELEASE: 1985

BILLBOARD CHART PERFORMANCE: #1 FOR 9 WEEKS,

   JUNE 8, 1985; 97 WEEKS ON CHARTS

SONGS

SO FAR AWAY

MONEY FOR NOTHING

WALK OF LIFE

YOUR LATEST TRICK

WHY WORRY

RIDE ACROSS THE RIVER

THE MAN'S TOO STRONG

ONE WORLD

BROTHERS IN ARMS

AJL1-5429

BE YOURSELF TONIGHT

RECORD COMPANY: RCA

CATALOG NUMBER: AJL1-5429

YEAR OF RELEASE: 1985

BILLBOARD CHART PERFORMANCE: #9, MAY 25, 1985;

 45 WEEKS ON CHARTS

EURYTHMICS

SONGS

WOULD I LIE TO YOU?

THERE MUST BE AN ANGEL (PLAYING WITH

MY HEART)

I LOVE YOU LIKE A BALL AND CHAIN

SISTERS ARE DOIN' IT FOR THEMSELVES

CONDITIONED SOUL

ADRIAN

IT'S ALRIGHT (BABY'S COMING BACK)

HERE COMES THAT SINKING FEELING

BETTER TO HAVE LOST IN LOVE (THAN NEVER TO

HAVE LOVED AT ALL)

The dream of the blue turtles

THE DREAM OF THE BLUE TURTLES

RECORD COMPANY: A&M

CATALOG NUMBER: SP-3750

YEAR OF RELEASE: 1985

BILLBOARD **CHART PERFORMANCE:** #2, JULY 13, 1985;
   58 WEEKS ON CHARTS

STING

SONGS

IF YOU LOVE SOMEBODY SET THEM FREE

LOVE IS THE SEVENTH WAVE

RUSSIANS

CHILDREN'S CRUSADE

SHADOWS IN THE RAIN

WE WORK THE BLACK SEAM

CONSIDER ME GONE

THE DREAM OF THE BLUE TURTLES

MOON OVER BOURBON STREET

FORTRESS AROUND YOUR HEART

SLIPPERY WHEN WET

RECORD COMPANY: MERCURY

CATALOG NUMBER: 820 264-1

YEAR OF RELEASE: 1986

BILLBOARD CHART PERFORMANCE: #1 FOR 8 WEEKS,

  SEPTEMBER 13, 1986; 94 WEEKS ON CHARTS

BON JOVI

SONGS

LET IT ROCK

YOU GIVE LOVE A BAD NAME

LIVIN' ON A PRAYER

SOCIAL DISEASE

WANTED DEAD OR ALIVE

RAISE YOUR HANDS

WITHOUT LOVE

I'D DIE FOR YOU

NEVER SAY GOODBYE

WILD IN THE STREETS

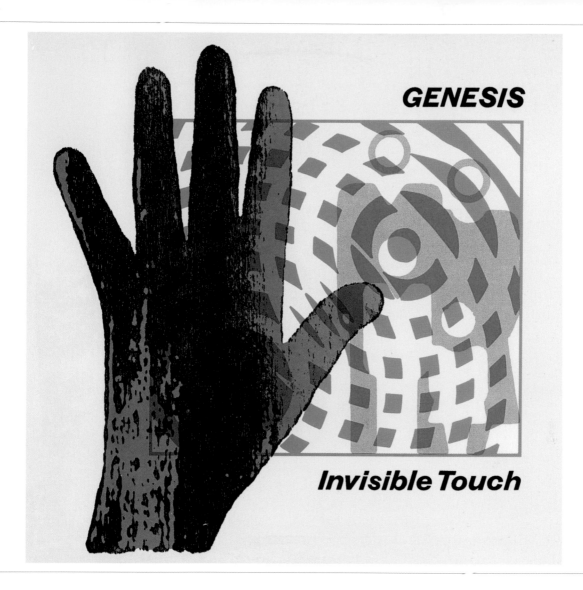

INVISIBLE TOUCH

RECORD COMPANY: ATLANTIC

CATALOG NUMBER: 81641-1-E

YEAR OF RELEASE: 1986

BILLBOARD CHART PERFORMANCE: #3, JUNE 28, 1986;

   85 WEEKS ON CHARTS

GENESIS

SONGS

INVISIBLE TOUCH

TONIGHT, TONIGHT, TONIGHT

LAND OF CONFUSION

IN TOO DEEP

ANYTHING SHE DOES

DOMINO:

PART ONE - IN THE GLOW OF THE NIGHT

PART TWO - THE LAST DOMINO

THROWING IT ALL AWAY

THE BRAZILIAN

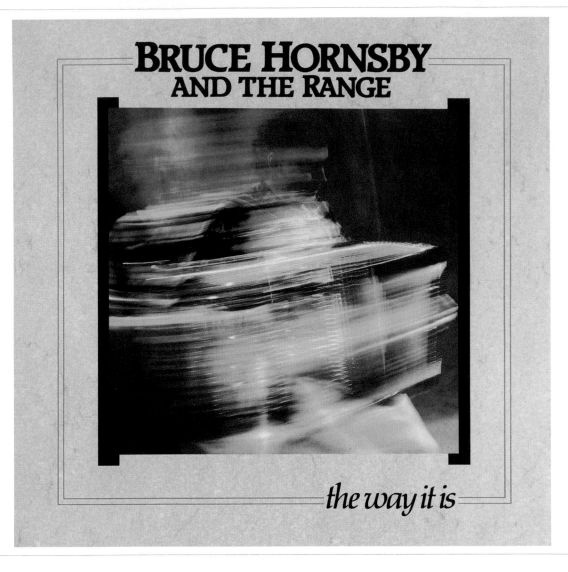

THE WAY IT IS

RECORD COMPANY: RCA

CATALOG NUMBER: NFL1-8058

YEAR OF RELEASE: 1986

BILLBOARD CHART PERFORMANCE: #3, JUNE 21, 1986;

  73 WEEKS ON CHARTS

BRUCE HORNSBY AND THE RANGE

SONGS

ON THE WESTERN SKYLINE

EVERY LITTLE KISS

MANDOLIN RAIN

THE LONG RACE

THE WAY IT IS

DOWN THE ROAD TONIGHT

THE WILD FRONTIER

THE RIVER RUNS LOW

THE RED PLAINS

CONTROL

RECORD COMPANY: A&M

CATALOG NUMBER: SP-3905

YEAR OF RELEASE: 1986

BILLBOARD CHART PERFORMANCE: #1 FOR 2 WEEKS,

   MARCH 8, 1986; 106 WEEKS ON CHARTS

JANET JACKSON

SONGS

CONTROL

NASTY

WHAT HAVE YOU DONE FOR ME LATELY

YOU CAN BE MINE

THE PLEASURE PRINCIPLE

WHEN I THINK OF YOU

HE DOESN'T KNOW I'M ALIVE

LET'S WAIT AWHILE

FUNNY HOW TIME FLIES (WHEN YOU'RE

HAVING FUN)

FORE!

RECORD COMPANY: CHRYSALIS

CATALOG NUMBER: OV 41534

YEAR OF RELEASE: 1986

BILLBOARD CHART PERFORMANCE: #1 FOR ONE WEEK,

SEPTEMBER 13, 1986; 61 WEEKS ON CHARTS

HUEY LEWIS AND THE NEWS

SONGS

JACOB'S LADDER

STUCK WITH YOU

WHOLE LOTTA LOVIN'

DOING IT ALL FOR MY BABY

HIP TO BE SQUARE

I KNOW WHAT I LIKE

I NEVER WALK ALONE

FOREST FOR THE TREES

NATURALLY

SIMPLE AS THAT

NOTE: THE SONG "THE POWER OF LOVE," FEATURED IN *THE TIME-LIFE MUSIC GOLD & PLATINUM COLLECTION,* APPEARS ONLY ON THE SOUNDTRACK FOR THE FILM *BACK TO THE FUTURE.*

5150

RECORD COMPANY: WARNER

CATALOG NUMBER: 25394

YEAR OF RELEASE: 1986

BILLBOARD CHART PERFORMANCE: #1 FOR 3 WEEKS,
   APRIL 12, 1986; 64 WEEKS ON CHARTS

VAN HALEN

SONGS

GOOD ENOUGH

WHY CAN'T THIS BE LOVE

GET UP

DREAMS

SUMMER NIGHTS

BEST OF BOTH WORLDS

LOVE WALKS IN

5150

INSIDE

Steve Winwood / Back in the High Life

BACK IN THE HIGH LIFE

RECORD COMPANY: ISLAND

CATALOG NUMBER: 9-25448

YEAR OF RELEASE: 1986

BILLBOARD CHART PERFORMANCE: #3, JULY 19, 1986;

   86 WEEKS ON CHARTS

STEVE WINWOOD

SONGS

HIGHER LOVE

TAKE IT AS IT COMES

FREEDOM OVERSPILL

BACK IN THE HIGH LIFE AGAIN

THE FINER THINGS

WAKE ME UP ON JUDGMENT DAY

SPLIT DECISION

MY LOVE'S LEAVIN'

HYSTERIA

RECORD COMPANY: MERCURY/POLYGRAM

CATALOG NUMBER: 830 675-1 Q

YEAR OF RELEASE: 1987

BILLBOARD CHART PERFORMANCE: #1 FOR 6 WEEKS,

    AUGUST 22, 1987; 133 WEEKS ON CHARTS

DEF LEPPARD

SONGS

WOMEN

ROCKET

ANIMAL

LOVE BITES

POUR SOME SUGAR ON ME

ARMAGEDDON IT

GODS OF WAR

DON'T SHOOT SHOTGUN

RUN RIOT

HYSTERIA

EXCITABLE

LOVE AND AFFECTION

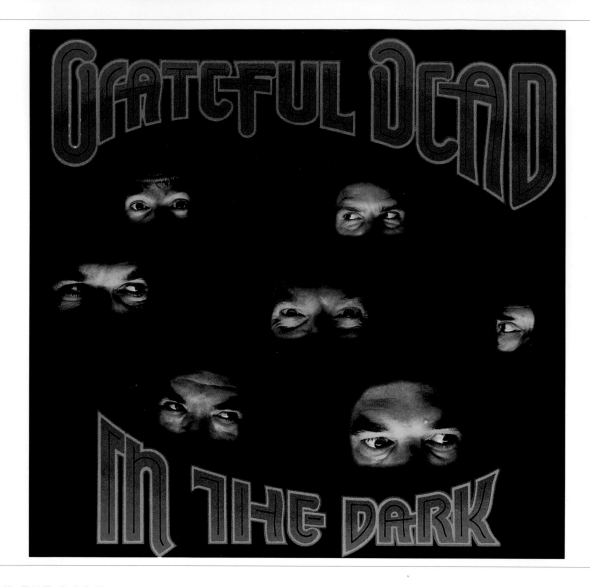

IN THE DARK

RECORD COMPANY: ARISTA

CATALOG NUMBER: AL-8452

YEAR OF RELEASE: 1987

BILLBOARD CHART PERFORMANCE: #6, JULY 25, 1987;

   34 WEEKS ON CHARTS

GRATEFUL DEAD

SONGS

TOUCH OF GREY

HELL IN A BUCKET

WHEN PUSH COMES TO SHOVE

WEST L.A. FADEAWAY

TONS OF STEEL

THROWING STONES

BLACK MUDDY RIVER

KICK

RECORD COMPANY: ATLANTIC

CATALOG NUMBER: 7 81796

YEAR OF RELEASE: 1987

BILLBOARD CHART PERFORMANCE: #3, NOVEMBER 14, 1987;

  81 WEEKS ON CHARTS

INXS

SONGS

GUNS IN THE SKY

NEW SENSATION

DEVIL INSIDE

NEED YOU TONIGHT

MEDIATE

THE LOVED ONE

WILD LIFE

NEVER TEAR US APART

MYSTIFY

KICK

CALLING ALL NATIONS

TINY DAGGERS

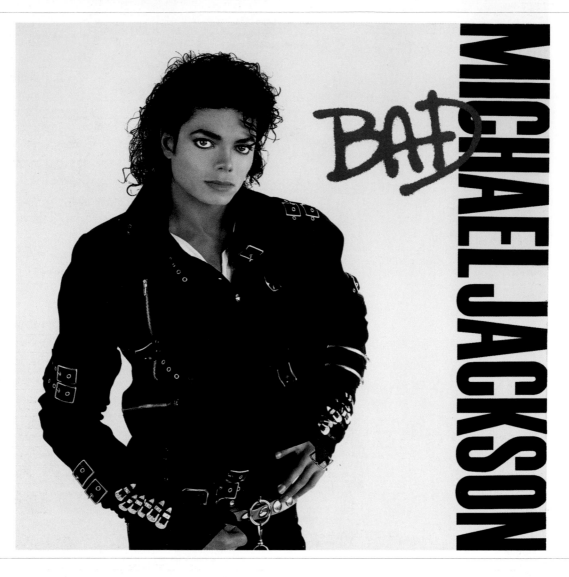

BAD

RECORD COMPANY: EPIC

CATALOG NUMBER: OE 40600

YEAR OF RELEASE: 1987

BILLBOARD CHART PERFORMANCE: #1 FOR 6 WEEKS,
    SEPTEMBER 26, 1987; 87 WEEKS ON CHARTS

MICHAEL JACKSON

SONGS

BAD

THE WAY YOU MAKE ME FEEL

SPEED DEMON

LIBERIAN GIRL

JUST GOOD FRIENDS

ANOTHER PART OF ME

MAN IN THE MIRROR

I JUST CAN'T STOP LOVING YOU

DIRTY DIANA

SMOOTH CRIMINAL

FAITH

GEORGE MICHAEL

RECORD COMPANY: COLUMBIA

CATALOG NUMBER: OC 40867

YEAR OF RELEASE: 1987

BILLBOARD CHART PERFORMANCE: #1 FOR 12 WEEKS,
 NOVEMBER 21, 1987; 87 WEEKS ON CHARTS

SONGS

FAITH

FATHER FIGURE

I WANT YOUR SEX

ONE MORE TRY

HARD DAY

HAND TO MOUTH

LOOK AT YOUR HANDS

MONKEY

KISSING A FOOL

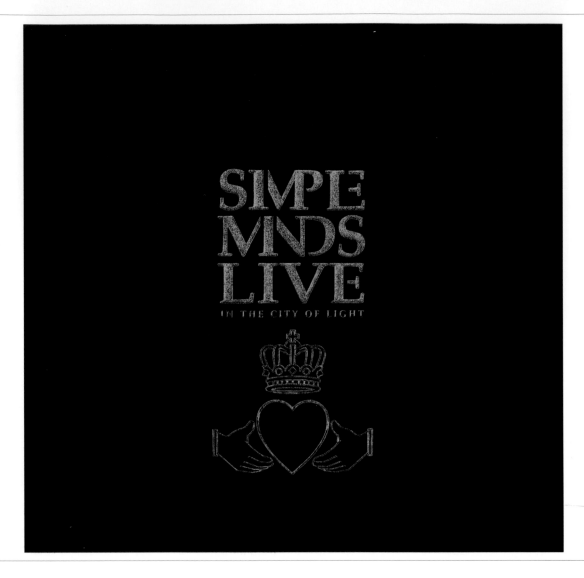

LIVE IN THE CITY OF LIGHT

RECORD COMPANY: VIRGIN/A&M

CATALOG NUMBER: SP 6850

YEAR OF RELEASE: 1987

BILLBOARD CHART PERFORMANCE: #96, JULY 18, 1987;

10 WEEKS ON CHARTS

SIMPLE MINDS

SONGS

GHOSTDANCING

BIG SLEEP

WATERFRONT

PROMISED YOU A MIRACLE

SOMEONE SOMEWHERE (IN SUMMERTIME)

OH JUNGLELAND

ALIVE AND KICKING

DON'T YOU (FORGET ABOUT ME)

ONCE UPON A TIME

BOOK OF BRILLIANT THINGS

EAST AT EASTER

SANCTIFY YOURSELF

LOVE SONG - SUN CITY - DANCE TO THE MUSIC

NEW GOLD DREAM

THE JOSHUA TREE

U 2

RECORD COMPANY: ISLAND

CATALOG NUMBER: 7 90581

YEAR OF RELEASE: 1987

BILLBOARD CHART PERFORMANCE: #1 FOR 9 WEEKS,

   APRIL 4, 1987; 103 WEEKS ON CHARTS

SONGS

WHERE THE STREETS HAVE NO NAME

I STILL HAVEN'T FOUND WHAT I'M LOOKING FOR

WITH OR WITHOUT YOU

BULLET THE BLUE SKY

RUNNING TO STAND STILL

RED HILL MINING TOWN

IN GOD'S COUNTRY

TRIP THROUGH YOUR WIRES

ONE TREE HILL

EXIT

MOTHERS OF THE DISAPPEARED

COSMIC THING

RECORD COMPANY: REPRISE

CATALOG NUMBER: 9 25854

YEAR OF RELEASE: 1989

BILLBOARD CHART PERFORMANCE: #4, JULY 22, 1989;

  65 WEEKS ON CHARTS

THE B-52'S

SONGS

COSMIC THING

DRY COUNTY

DEADBEAT CLUB

LOVE SHACK

JUNEBUG

ROAM

BUSHFIRE

CHANNEL Z

TOPAZ

FOLLOW YOUR BLISS

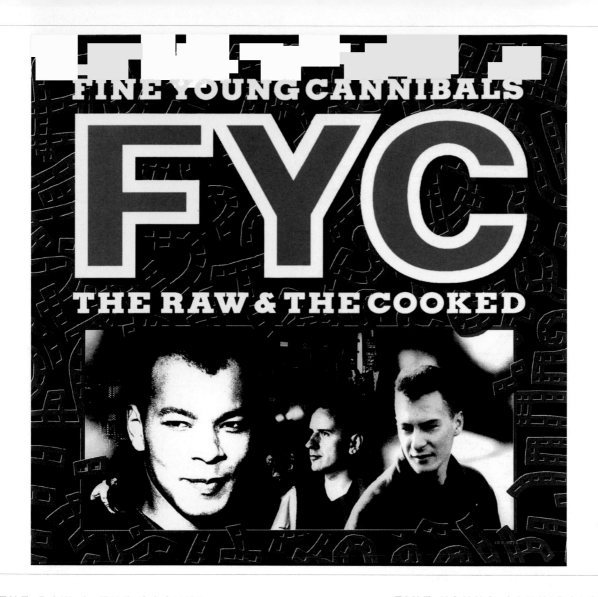

THE RAW & THE COOKED

RECORD COMPANY: I. R. S.

CATALOG NUMBER: 6273

YEAR OF RELEASE: 1989

BILLBOARD CHART PERFORMANCE: #1 FOR 7 WEEKS,

   MARCH 11, 1989; 63 WEEKS ON CHARTS

FINE YOUNG CANNIBALS

SONGS

SHE DRIVES ME CRAZY

GOOD THING

I'M NOT THE MAN I USED TO BE

I'M NOT SATISFIED

TELL ME WHAT

DON'T LOOK BACK

IT'S OK (IT'S ALRIGHT)

DON'T LET IT GET YOU DOWN

AS HARD AS IT IS

EVER FALLEN IN LOVE

THE END OF THE INNOCENCE

THE END OF THE INNOCENCE

RECORD COMPANY: GEFFEN

CATALOG NUMBER: GHS 24217

YEAR OF RELEASE: 1989

BILLBOARD CHART PERFORMANCE: #8, JULY 15, 1989;

   148 WEEKS ON CHARTS

DON HENLEY

SONGS

THE END OF THE INNOCENCE

HOW BAD DO YOU WANT IT?

I WILL NOT GO QUIETLY

THE LAST WORTHLESS EVENING

NEW YORK MINUTE

SHANGRI-LA

LITTLE TIN GOD

GIMME WHAT YOU GOT

IF DIRT WERE DOLLARS

THE HEART OF THE MATTER

LIKE A PRAYER

RECORD COMPANY: SIRE

CATALOG NUMBER: 25844

YEAR OF RELEASE: 1989

BILLBOARD CHART PERFORMANCE: #1 FOR 6 WEEKS,
   APRIL 8, 1989; 77 WEEKS ON CHARTS

MADONNA

tears for fears the seeds of love

SOWING THE SEEDS OF LOVE

RECORD COMPANY: FONTANA/POLYGRAM

CATALOG NUMBER: P2 38730

YEAR OF RELEASE: 1989

BILLBOARD CHART PERFORMANCE: #8, OCTOBER 7, 1989;

   34 WEEKS ON CHARTS

TEARS FOR FEARS

SONGS

WOMAN IN CHAINS

BADMAN'S SONG

SOWING THE SEEDS OF LOVE

ADVICE FOR THE YOUNG AT HEART

STANDING ON THE CORNER OF THE THIRD WORLD

SWORDS AND KNIVES

YEAR OF THE KNIFE

FAMOUS LAST WORDS

the

o question about it, music came primarily on CDs now. But the spatial limitations of the CD package, now accepted by album designers as the norm, actually inspired some interesting solutions. R.E.M.'s *Out of Time* is readable from a mile away, and the art director for Bonnie Raitt's *Luck of the Draw* calls attention to the title and artist simply by making sure nothing else gets in the way. Oddly enough, the oversized design for Sheryl Crow's *Tuesday Night Music Club* reads better in the smaller CD format than it would have on a twelve-inch-square LP jacket.

One of pop music's fragmented audiences preferred "classic rock"—hits and album tracks from earlier decades. And some designers hearkened back to the comfort of previous eras even for new releases: The Smashing Pumpkins' *Mellon Collie and the Infinite Sadness* would fit perfectly in a group of albums from the sixties.

Ironically, a band that sounded like it belonged to a previous era sported one of the decade's most distinctive designs. On Hootie and the Blowfish's *Cracked Rear View,* blurry snapshots obscured any literal meaning, while the straight-ahead music inside made the album a huge hit. And 10,000 Maniacs' *Our Time in Eden* finds some humor by using artwork from antiquity set against a very plain type treatment spelling out the band's unusual name.

The evolution of album design is still going on, as graphic artists experiment with new ways to get the music noticed. And they'll find them. These days you don't flip an album over to get more information while you're listening, you pull out a little booklet. But album images will continue to attach themselves to pop music, because the great pop tradition of outstanding design has taught us something wonderful: how to listen with our eyes.

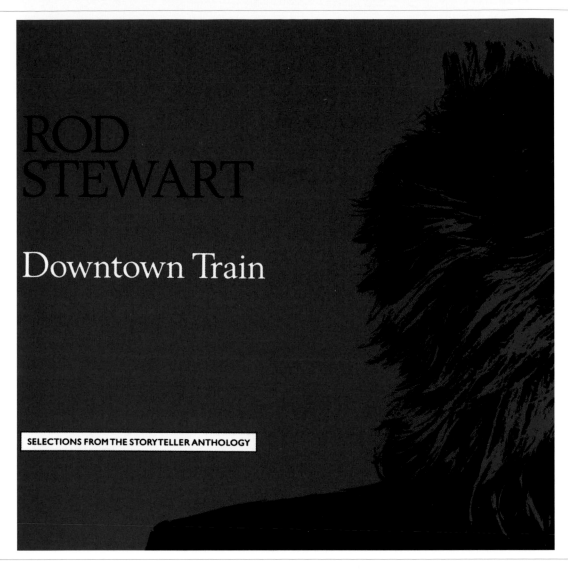

ROD STEWART

Downtown Train

SELECTIONS FROM THE STORYTELLER ANTHOLOGY

DOWNTOWN TRAIN   ROD STEWART

RECORD COMPANY: WARNER

CATALOG NUMBER: 9 26158

YEAR OF RELEASE: 1990

BILLBOARD CHART PERFORMANCE: #20, APRIL 7, 1990;

   12 WEEKS ON CHARTS*

SONGS

STAY WITH ME

TONIGHT'S THE NIGHT

(GONNA BE ALRIGHT)

THE KILLING OF GEORGIE

(PART I AND II)

PASSION

YOUNG TURKS

INFATUATION

PEOPLE GET READY

FOREVER YOUNG

MY HEART CAN'T TELL YOU NO

I DON'T WANT TO TALK ABOUT IT

(1989 VERSION)

DOWNTOWN TRAIN

*THIS ALBUM IS AVAILABLE ON ITS OWN, BUT IS ALSO DISK 4 FROM THE 4 DISK
THE STORYTELLER ANTHOLOGY.

LUCK OF THE DRAW

RECORD COMPANY: CAPITOL

CATALOG NUMBER: C2-96111

YEAR OF RELEASE: 1991

BILLBOARD CHART PERFORMANCE: #2, JULY 13, 1991;

    120 WEEKS ON CHARTS

BONNIE RAITT

SONGS

SOMETHING TO TALK ABOUT

GOOD MAN, GOOD WOMAN

I CAN'T MAKE YOU LOVE ME

TANGLED AND DARK

COME TO ME

NO BUSINESS

ONE PART BE MY LOVER

NOT THE ONLY ONE

PAPA COME QUICK (JODY AND CHICO)

SLOW RIDE

LUCK OF THE DRAW

ALL AT ONCE

OUT OF TIME

RECORD COMPANY: WARNER

CATALOG NUMBER: 9 26496

YEAR OF RELEASE: 1991

BILLBOARD CHART PERFORMANCE: #1 FOR 2 WEEKS,

   MARCH 30, 1991; 109 WEEKS ON CHARTS

R . E . M .

SONGS

RADIO SONG

LOSING MY RELIGION

LOW

NEAR WILD HEAVEN

ENDGAME

SHINY HAPPY PEOPLE

BELONG

HALF A WORLD AWAY

TEXARKANA

COUNTRY FEEDBACK

ME IN HONEY

THE ONE

RECORD COMPANY: MCA

CATALOG NUMBER: 10614

YEAR OF RELEASE: 1992

BILLBOARD CHART PERFORMANCE: #8, JULY 11, 1992;

    26 WEEKS ON CHARTS

ELTON JOHN

SONGS

SIMPLE LIFE

THE ONE

SWEAT IT OUT

RUNAWAY TRAIN

WHITEWASH COUNTY

THE NORTH

WHEN A WOMAN DOESN'T WANT YOU

EMILY

ON DARK STREET

UNDERSTANDING WOMEN

THE LAST SONG

10,000 Maniacs

Our Time In Eden

OUR TIME IN EDEN

RECORD COMPANY: ELEKTRA

CATALOG NUMBER: 961385

YEAR OF RELEASE: 1992

BILLBOARD CHART PERFORMANCE: #28, OCTOBER 17, 1992;

   56 WEEKS ON CHARTS

10,000 MANIACS

SONGS

NOAH'S DOVE

THESE ARE DAYS

EDEN

FEW AND FAR BETWEEN

STOCKTON GALA DAYS

GOLD RUSH BRIDES

JEZEBEL

HOW YOU'VE GROWN

CANDY EVERYBODY WANTS

TOLERANCE

CIRCLE DREAM

IF YOU INTEND

I'M NOT THE MAN

COOLEYHIGHHARMONY [REMIXES]

BOYZ II MEN

RECORD COMPANY: MOTOWN

CATALOG NUMBER: 314-530231

YEAR OF RELEASE: 1993

BILLBOARD CHART PERFORMANCE: #154, JANUARY 8, 1994;
  6 WEEKS ON CHARTS

SONGS

AL FINAL DEL CAMINO
(END OF THE ROAD,
SPANISH VERSION)

PLEASE DON'T GO

LONELY HEART

THIS IS MY HEART

UHH AHH (SEQUEL VERSION)

IT'S SO HARD TO SAY
GOODBYE TO YESTERDAY
(ORIGINAL VERSION)

IN THE STILL OF THE NIGHT
(I'LL REMEMBER)

MOTOWNPHILLY
(REMIX RADIO EDIT)

UNDER PRESSURE

SYMPIN (REMIX RADIO EDIT)

LITTLE THINGS

YOUR LOVE

MOTOWNPHILLY
(ORIGINAL VERSION)

SYMPIN (ORIGINAL VERSION)

UHH AHH (ORIGINAL VERSION)

ITS SO HARD TO SAY

GOODBYE TO YESTERDAY
(RADIO VERSION)

END OF THE ROAD
(LP VERSION)

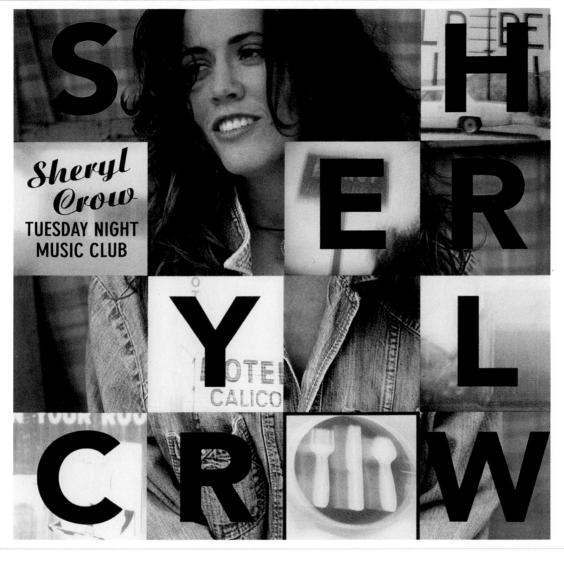

TUESDAY NIGHT MUSIC CLUB

RECORD COMPANY: A&M

CATALOG NUMBER: 31454 0126

YEAR OF RELEASE: 1993

BILLBOARD CHART PERFORMANCE: #8, MARCH 19, 1994;

  100 WEEKS ON CHARTS

SHERYL CROW

SONGS

RUN, BABY, RUN

LEAVING LAS VEGAS

STRONG ENOUGH

CAN'T CRY ANYMORE

SOLIDIFY

THE NA-NA SONG

NO ONE SAID IT WOULD BE EASY

WHAT CAN I DO FOR YOU

ALL I WANNA DO

WE DO WHAT WE CAN

I SHALL BELIEVE

124

BAT OUT OF HELL II: BACK INTO HELL

MEAT LOAF

RECORD COMPANY: MCA

CATALOG NUMBER: MCAD-10699

YEAR OF RELEASE: 1993

BILLBOARD CHART PERFORMANCE: #1 FOR ONE WEEK,
 OCTOBER 2, 1993; 55 WEEKS ON CHARTS

SONGS

I'D DO ANYTHING FOR LOVE (BUT I WON'T DO THAT)

LIFE IS A LEMON AND I WANT MY MONEY BACK

ROCK AND ROLL DREAMS COME THROUGH

IT JUST WON'T QUIT

OUT OF THE FRYING PAN (AND INTO THE FIRE)

OBJECTS IN THE REAR VIEW MIRROR MAY APPEAR

CLOSER THAN THEY ARE

WASTED YOUTH

EVERYTHING LOUDER THAN EVERYTHING ELSE

GOOD GIRLS GO TO HEAVEN (BAD GIRLS

GO EVERYWHERE)

BACK INTO HELL

LOST BOYS AND GOLDEN GIRLS

CRACKED REAR VIEW

RECORD COMPANY: ATLANTIC

CATALOG NUMBER: 82613

YEAR OF RELEASE: 1994

BILLBOARD CHART PERFORMANCE: #1 FOR 8 WEEKS,

   JULY 23, 1994; 129 WEEKS ON CHARTS

HOOTIE AND THE BLOWFISH

SONGS

HANNAH JANE

HOLD MY HAND

LET HER CRY

ONLY WANNA BE WITH YOU

RUNNING FROM AN ANGEL

I'M GOIN' HOME

DROWNING

TIME

LOOK AWAY

NOT EVEN THE TREES

GOODBYE

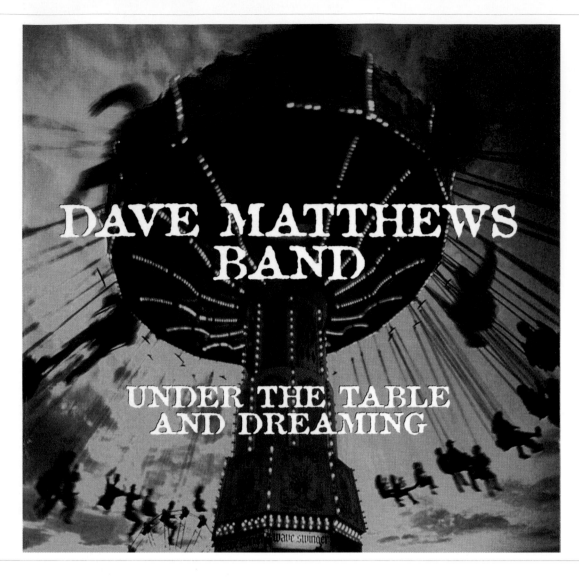

UNDER THE TABLE AND DREAMING

RECORD COMPANY: RCA

CATALOG NUMBER: 07863 66449

YEAR OF RELEASE: 1995

BILLBOARD CHART PERFORMANCE: #11, OCTOBER 15, 1995;

   102 WEEK ON CHARTS

DAVE MATTHEWS BAND

SONGS

THE BEST OF WHAT'S AROUND

WHAT WOULD YOU SAY

SATELLITE

RHYME AND REASON

TYPICAL SITUATION

DANCING NANCIES

ANTS MARCHING

LOVER LAY DOWN

JIMI THING

WAREHOUSE

PAY FOR WHAT YOU GET

#34

MELLON COLLIE AND THE INFINITE SADNESS   SMASHING PUMPKINS

RECORD COMPANY: VIRGIN

CATALOG NUMBER: 40861-2

YEAR OF RELEASE: 1995

BILLBOARD CHART PERFORMANCE: #1 FOR ONE WEEK,
   NOVEMBER 11, 1995; 89 WEEKS ON CHARTS

SONGS

DAWN TO DUSK	TWILIGHT TO STARLIGHT
MELLON COLLIE AND THE	WHERE THE BOYS FEAR
INFINITE SADNESS	TO TREAD
TONIGHT, TONIGHT	BODIES
JELLYBELLY	THIRTY-THREE
ZERO	IN THE ARMS OF SLEEP
HERE IS NO WHY	1979
BULLET WITH BUTTERFLY WINGS	TALES OF A SCORCHED EARTH
TO FORGIVE	THRU THE EYES OF RUBY
AN ODE TO NO ONE	STUMBLEINE
LOVE	X.Y.U.
CUPID DE LOCKE	WE ONLY COME OUT AT NIGHT
GALAPAGOS	BEAUTIFUL
MUZZLE	LILY (MY ONE AND ONLY)
PORCELINA OF THE VAST OCEANS	BY STARLIGHT
TAKE ME DOWN	FAREWELL AND GOODNIGHT